Frederick V. Coville

Forest Growth and Sheep Grazing in the Cascade Mountains

of Oregon

Frederick V. Coville

Forest Growth and Sheep Grazing in the Cascade Mountains of Oregon

ISBN/EAN: 9783337317461

Printed in Europe, USA, Canada, Australia, Japan

Cover: Foto ©Andreas Hilbeck / pixelio.de

More available books at **www.hansebooks.com**

U. S. DEPARTMENT OF AGRICULTURE

DIVISION OF FORESTRY.

!

FOREST GROWTH AND SHEEP GRAZING

IN THE CASCADE MOUNTAINS OF OREGON.

BY

FREDERICK V. COVILLE.

WASHINGTON:
GOVERNMENT PRINTING OFFICE.
1898.

BULLETIN No. 15.

U. S. DEPARTMENT OF AGRICULTURE.

DIVISION OF FORESTRY.

FOREST GROWTH AND SHEEP GRAZING

IN THE CASCADE MOUNTAINS OF OREGON.

BY

FREDERICK V. COVILLE.

WASHINGTON:

GOVERNMENT PRINTING OFFICE.

1898.

LETTER OF TRANSMITTAL.

—

U. S. Department of Agriculture,
Division of Forestry,
Washington, D. C., February 8, 1898.

Sir: Mr. Frederick V. Coville, Botanist of the Department, while engaged in an extended botanical exploration of the Pacific Coast region, during the summer of 1897 incidentally made observations regarding the effect of sheep grazing on forest growth in the Cascade Range Forest Reserve, which he has fully recorded in the accompanying report.

Believing that the problems discussed are more germane to those with which the Division of Forestry should deal, than to botanical questions, he has turned over the same to this division.

I recommend that the report be printed without delay, since this question has an important bearing upon the forest policy of the General Government and has been here most lucidly and exhaustively treated.

I indorse fully Mr. Coville's conclusions that sheep grazing without proper restrictions and regulations, which have in view to prevent overstocking, is detrimental to the reproduction of forest growth and to soil conditions and water flow—in some localities more so than in others; hence, wherever forest growth is to be maintained and the washing of soils with consequent flood dangers is to be avoided, the greatest care and judgment must be exercised as to the manner in which sheep grazing may be carried on without detriment.

I take this opportunity to express the thanks of the division to Mr. Coville for placing this valuable information at its disposal.

Respectfully,

B. E. Fernow, *Chief.*

Hon. James Wilson, *Secretary.*

3

CONTENTS

FOREST GROWTH AND SHEEP GRAZING IN THE CASCADE MOUNTAINS OF OREGON.

INTRODUCTION.

For the past few years a bitter controversy has been waged in Oregon on the question of grazing sheep in the Cascade Range Forest Reserve. Recent legislation by Congress has made it necessary to devise a series of regulations regarding this industry, and in the face of a great deal of diametrically conflicting testimony regarding the effect of sheep grazing, the Interior Department felt the need of a disinterested investigation of the facts before formulating any detailed set of rules. The aid of the Department of Agriculture was solicited, and the result of the investigation is here presented. A preliminary report was transmitted to the Secretary of the Interior on November 22, 1897.[1]

Hon. Binger Hermann, Commissioner of the General Land Office, furnished the writer with valuable letters of introduction to several prominent citizens of Oregon, who were familiar with the sheep grazing question. Mr. John Minto, of Salem, Oreg., gave a general letter of introduction to the sheepmen of eastern Oregon which made it possible to secure a large amount of information through channels that ordinarily would have been closed to a Government officer investigating this subject. Among the many others whose courtesy contributed materially to the success of the investigation should be mentioned particularly Mr. Thomas Cooper and Mr. E. F. Benson of the western land office of the Northern Pacific Railroad, at Tacoma, Wash., who have recently been conducting an investigation of sheep grazing on the railroad lands.

An outfit was procured at Klamath Falls, in the southern part of Oregon, and the party, consisting of the writer, Mr. E. I. Applegate, acting as assistant, and a camp hand, with three saddle horses and five pack horses, entered the southern end of the reserve on July 23. From this time until September 6, when we reached The Dalles on the Columbia River at the northern end of the reserve, a thorough examination of the forests was made, including not only those portions in which sheep now graze but other typical portions in which sheep have never grazed. We traversed, besides the well known parts of the Cascades, some of the most remote and inaccessible portions, where traveling largely without trails, we interviewed sheep owners, packers, and

---

[1] A copy of the present report was transmitted to the Interior Department on January 21, 1898.

herders, cattle owners, and all classes of people; both those who favored and those who were opposed to the permitting of sheep grazing within the reserve. We followed the bands of sheep as they were grazing, watched their movements, their choice of forage, and the methods of handling them; observed the effects both of recent grazing and of the grazing of former years; and investigated the devastation caused by fires. Areas of the forests were examined in every stage, from total immunity from fires to total destruction by them. Many fires were burning, and whenever possible the exact cause was ascertained.

Four detours were made from the mountains down into the plains at their eastern base to consult with sheep owners and other well-informed citizens, the longest being a trip by the writer from Sisters to Prineville and thence to Sherar Bridge, August 26 to 30, Mr. Applegate meanwhile prosecuting the investigations in the mountains.

THE SHEEP INDUSTRY OF OREGON.

The first domesticated sheep brought into Oregon came from California in 1843, but from that year until 1860 sheep raising was only a small industry. About the latter date, however, wool began to assume considerable importance in the region as an agricultural product. The following table, taken chiefly from the United States census reports, gives some idea of the growth and importance of the sheep industry in Oregon:

Pounds of wool produced in Oregon in census years.

1850	29,686
1860	219,012
1870	1,080,638
1880	5,718,524
1890	9,982,910
1895 [1]	12,038,091

The following table, compiled from the reports of the Division of Statistics, shows the amount of money invested in sheep in the State of Oregon each year since 1870:

Growth of the sheep industry in Oregon.

Year.	Number of sheep.	Value of sheep.	Year.	Number of sheep.	Value of sheep.
1870	500,000	$950,000	1884	2,571,378	$4,654,194
1871	419,200	796,480	1885	2,519,950	4,057,120
1872	4e6,200	1,191,190	1886	2,469,551	3,618,139
1873	534,800	1,476,048	1887	2,593,029	3,670,173
1874	561,500	1,403,750	1888	2,930,123	4,987,069
1875	634,400	1,643,006	1889	2,959,424	5,105,894
1876	710,500	1,413,895	1890	2,929,830	5,622,344
1877	859,700	1,547,460	1891	2,431,759	5,154,114
1878	1,074,600	1,891,296	1892	2,456,077	5,491,789
1879	1,160,600	1,822,142	1893	2,456,077	5,903,182
1880	1,265,100	1,847,046	1894	2,529,750	4,433,403
1881	1,176,433	1,717,592	1895	2,529,759	2,945,905
1882	2,333,162	3,733,059	1896	2,630,949	3,590,983
1883	2,403,157	5,166,788	1897	2,604,640	3,459,222

[1] From the Oregon State census report for 1895.

Following the general progress of agricultural settlement, sheep raising in Oregon was carried on first in the Willamette Valley, in the western portion of the State, later in the Grand Ronde, in extreme northeastern Oregon, and then, crowded out of these fertile places by the more profitable occupations of agriculture proper, the sheep owners moved their flocks to more and more remote parts of the State, especially to the great sage plains in its eastern portion, where the ordinary processes of agriculture are confined to small areas, chiefly irrigated land, and the country is for the most part so dry as to be adapted only for grazing.

The distinction between range sheep and farm sheep must be clearly understood. In a thickly settled agricultural region in which all or nearly all the land is cut up into farms, or ranches, as they are called in the western United States, it is a common practice to keep on each ranch a small number of sheep, from a few individuals to a few hundred. These are inclosed in fenced pastures and do not therefore require a herder. Range sheep, on the other hand, are pastured or grazed on the great areas of unfenced public or Government land, popularly known as the open range, the outside range, or simply the range. Because this land is not fenced, and because unprotected sheep would be liable to destruction by wild animals, especially coyotes or prairie wolves, these range sheep are accompanied and cared for by a man who is called a sheep herder, or simply a herder. As a matter of economy, each herder is intrusted with as many sheep as he can properly manage, commonly two or three thousand. Such an aggregation of sheep is called a band. The terms flock and shepherd are seldom heard in the range region of Oregon, and in this report, therefore, the term "band," in common use there, will be employed.

Twenty years ago the sheep that were owned on the treeless plains of eastern Oregon, at points remote from the forest-covered mountains, were pastured in fall, winter, and spring, just as they now are, upon the open range; but during the hot and dry summer months, when on the summits of the plateaus the grass tops were dead, water for the sheep was wanting, and the heat was oppressive, it became imperative that the sheep be kept in the bottoms of the deep, rock-walled canyons which form the drainage channels of the region. Here were found water, fresh grass, and shade, which carried the sheep through the summer in good condition. But as sheep raising, proving a profitable industry, became more popular it was found that these canyons, on account of their limited area, could furnish summer range for only a portion of the sheep that could readily find pasturage on the winter range. In order, therefore, to utilize more of the winter range it was necessary to increase the summer range, and this it was found possible to do by driving the sheep in late spring or early summer to some of the cool, well-watered, grassy, timber-covered mountains that adjoin the plains. By this modification of the yearly routine the possibilities of sheep raising on the plains were enormously increased. For example, that portion of the plains extending from Antelope to Bakeoven, in Wasco County, which, under the old system, could carry only 6,000 sheep, now carries 25,000 sheep.

SUMMER SHEEP GRAZING IN THE MOUNTAINS.

Outside an unimportant amount of grazing carried on in the vicinity of The Dalles as much as thirty years ago, the mountains first resorted to for summer range were the Blue Mountains, which are situated in the northeastern portion of the State and east of the principal sheep-grazing area of the plains. First, beginning about twenty-five years ago, only the lower slopes of the mountains were used, but little by little the increasing need of additional summer range forced the sheep farther and farther into the mountains and finally to their very summits.

The summer pasturage afforded by the Cascade Mountains to the west of the plains soon began to attract the attention of sheep owners. First the foothills, then the middle elevations, and finally the higher slopes were occupied, a condition which has existed since about 1886. A similar occupation of Gearhart, Warner, and other mountains in southern Oregon, south of the plains, has taken place within the past few years.

THE CASCADE RANGE FOREST RESERVE.

In the session of the Oregon State legislature for 1888–89 Judge John B. Waldo, of Macleay, a member of the legislature, introduced a joint memorial asking the Congress of the United States to set aside as a public reserve a certain specified tract in the Cascade Mountains. This memorial passed the Oregon house of representatives, but failed in the senate. The matter subsequently came up in the form of a petition to the President, and by an executive proclamation under date of September 28, 1893, the proposed lands were finally set aside as the Cascade Range Forest Reserve. This reserve, which contains 4,492,800 acres, extends in a north and south direction almost across the State, embracing the main ridge of the Cascades and a broad strip on either slope. It is about 235 miles long, with a width varying from 18 to 60 miles.

From the time the Cascade reserve was created there was a difference of opinion among the people of Oregon regarding the effect of sheep grazing within its limits, one party to the controversy maintaining that the sheep were a serious detriment to the interests for which the reserve was created, the other maintaining that they were not. The first official action taken by the Government was the issuing of regulations, under date of April 14, 1894, governing all the forest reserves, and, among other details, prohibiting the "driving, feeding, grazing, pasturing, or herding of cattle, sheep, or other live stock" within any of the reserves.

The effect of these regulations in excluding sheep from their customary summer grazing lands in the Cascades gave rise to vigorous and continued protests from those interested in the sheep industry. These protests finally resulted in a letter, under date of February 10, 1896, from the Oregon delegation in Congress to the Department of the Interior, recommending that in lieu of the present reserve three smaller reserves be made, about Mount Hood, Mount Jefferson, and Crater Lake, and that the balance of the Cascade reserve be thrown open. Action favorable to this recommendation, however, was never taken by the Department.

During the summer of 1896, under special instructions from the Attorney-General of the United States, dated January 10 of the same year, several arrests were made of sheep herders, sheep owners, and others grazing sheep on the reserve. Later these cases assumed the form of civil instead of criminal proceedings, and on September 3, 1896, suit was brought in the United States district court of Oregon against several owners to enjoin them from grazing within the reserve. These suits were pending for several months until, in May, 1897, the Attorney-General, in view of probable early legislative action by Congress involving a new scheme of administration of the reserves, issued instructions that the injunction suits be discontinued. On June 4, 1897, the expected legislation by Congress was approved by the President, in the form of a provision in the sundry civil appropriation act authorizing the Secretary of the Interior to make all necessary regulations for the government of the forest reserves.[1]

In a series of regulations governing the forest reserves, issued from the General Land Office under date of June 30, 1897, the following provisions are made:

The pasturing of live stock on the public lands in forest reservations will not be interfered with so long as it appears that injury is not being done to the forest growth, and the rights of others are not thereby jeopardized. The pasturing of sheep is, however, prohibited in all forest reservations, except those in the States of Oregon and Washington, for the reason that sheep grazing has been found injurious to the forest cover, and therefore of serious consequence in regions where the rainfall is limited. The exception in favor of the States of Oregon and Washington is made because the continuous moisture and abundant rainfall of the Cascade and Pacific coast ranges make rapid renewal of herbage and undergrowth possible. Owners of sheep are required to make application to the Commissioner of the General Land Office for permission to pasture, stating the number of sheep and the location on the reserves where it is desired to graze. Permission will be refused or revoked whenever it shall appear that sheep are pastured on parts of the reserves specially liable to injury, or upon and in the vicinity of the Bull Run reserve, Crater Lake, Mount Hood, Mount Rainier, or other well-known places of public resort or reservoir supply. Permission will also cease upon proof of neglect as to the care of fires made by herders, or of the violation by them of any of the forest-reserve regulations.

These regulations, however, were issued so late in the season that the provision regarding permits was ineffective for the summer of 1897, as those who pastured on the reserve had already entered it before the regulations had been issued.

---

[1] See a review of the subject in a letter from Binger Hermann, Commissioner of the General Land Office, to the Secretary of the Interior, published in the Portland Oregonian for May 23, 1897.

FACTS BROUGHT OUT BY THE INVESTIGATION.

CHARACTER OF THE PERSONS ENGAGED IN THE BUSINESS.

All the sheep owners in eastern Oregon appear to be American citizens; at least upon inquiry no aliens were found. Some of the owners, as with our farming population in all parts of the country, are of foreign birth, but have become naturalized. In earlier years, too, some of the herders were French or Portuguese. Many of the owners are prominent influential citizens of the highest character.

A popular impression seems to prevail that sheep herders in Oregon, as elsewhere, represent a comparatively low class of humanity. This impression as applied to the majority of sheep herders many years ago was perhaps correct. At the present time, however, many bright and reputable young men have undertaken sheep herding in default of opportunities for more desirable work, and as a whole they probably average as well in character as the men engaged in any other branch of agricultural industry.

COST OF MAINTAINING A BAND OF SHEEP.

Under present conditions a sheep owner with one or two bands can seldom conduct his business profitably if he follows a nomadic life, and in general it is a prerequisite of success that an owner shall have for winter headquarters a permanent and commodious, properly fenced ranch, provided with a house, one or more hay barns, and several substantial corrals. It must have enough arable land to grow the hay necessary for wintering his sheep. Such a ranch represents a capital of about $5,000 or $6,000. The following is a fair estimate of the cost of "running"—that is, maintaining—a band of 2,000 ewes for a year in a typical place in Sherman County:

Taxes, 21 mills per dollar, on an assessed valuation of $2 per head	$84
Herder, 12 months, at $30 per month.................................	360
Packer, 5 months, at $30 per month	150
"Grub"—that is, food provisions—for the herder and packer, at $10 per month each	170
Rental of winter range, 6 months	100
Shearing, at 5 cents per head......................................	100
Wheat hay, sufficient for 40 days, at the rate of 3 tons for 100 sheep, at $7 per ton	420
Salt, 100 pounds per week, at 50 cents per 100, plus $1 per 100 for freighting to summer range during 20 weeks	46
Hauling wool to the railroad, at 40 cents per 100 pounds, the estimated clip being 8 pounds per sheep	64
Extra help for 1 month during the lambing season, at the rate of 1 man for 200 ewes, at a salary of $30 per month.................................	300
Outfit for herder and packer, including horses, pack saddles, tent, and bedding..	25
Bucks, at the rate of 2 bucks per 100 ewes, replaced every 2 years, at an average cost of $10 each	200
Summering bucks, which are kept separate from the ewe bands, at $1 each..	40
Total	2,059

13

The actual annual expenditure on a band of sheep, of course, varies with many conditions, such as the distance of the ranch from a railroad, the owner raising his own hay, or acting as his own packer, the necessity of renting private range, the size of the band, etc., but in general the estimated cost of running sheep is 75 cents to $1 per head. Sheep owners are accustomed to estimate that the cost of running a band of sheep will be paid by the sale of the wool, while the increase represents probable profits.

Sometimes sheep are leased, the annual rental varying from 40 cents to $1 per head, according to the condition of the wool and mutton market, the lessee returning to the owner as many ewes as he received and taking the increase as part of his profits. Sometimes, particularly when the lessee is a young man getting a start in the business, the rental paid is half the wool and half the increase.

The sheep of eastern Oregon are chiefly of Merino stock, but the increasing profitableness of good mutton sheep has induced many of the owners to introduce Shropshire blood. This movement appears to be successful, particularly with careful management of the bands. An annual increase of 90 per cent to 100 per cent is quite feasible and is actually secured by sound methods, where careless methods give an increase of only 50 per cent to 60 per cent.

YEARLY ROUTINE IN HANDLING SHEEP.

The yearly routine of a band up to the time of starting for the mountains in the spring may be given briefly as follows. When the sheep are brought back in the autumn from their summer range during the month of October, the bands are readjusted, the breeding ewes going in one group, the wethers, lambs, and dry ewes in another. For about a month, usually beginning between October 20 and November 1, the bucks are allowed to run with the ewes. They are herded on range land near the owner's ranch, seldom going more than a day's drive from headquarters. At this season the fall rains have started the grass and often a luxuriant growth takes place before it is checked by the cold of winter. When the snow storms begin, commonly toward the middle of December, the sheep are kept within corrals at the ranch and fed upon hay. The snow lies upon the ground for a period varying from six to forty days, according to season and elevation. When the snow has disappeared, the same system of ranging is pursued as in the autumn, until about the middle of March, when the lambing season begins. The period of gestation is twenty-one weeks. The lambing continues for about a month. After all the lambs are yeaned and the males castrated, the shearing of the adults begins, and keeps up until it is time to start for the mountains. The shearing is done on the ranch and the wool afterwards hauled to the shipping point. The practice, common in some regions, of driving the sheep to the shipping point and shearing them there is not generally followed in the Oregon plains.

Between May 15 and the end of the first week in June, when the grass of the plains begins to dry up, the bands, again readjusted (ewes and lambs together) and commonly varying in number from 1,800 to 2,700, the average being about 2,200, are driven toward the mountains. The average rate of travel is about 8 miles per day, varying with the heat, the feed, and the watering places. The usual practice is to start a band early, between daylight and sunrise, and let them travel slowly, grazing as they go, until about 9 o'clock. They then lie down, during the warmer part of the day, until 3 or 4 o'clock in the afternoon, when they start again and go on till sundown or a little later. They are watered once a day, if possible. Seldom earlier than the 10th of June and seldom later than the 1st of July they reach their summer range in the timber.

The bucks are kept in summer in inclosed pastures, or sometimes when an owner has a large enough number to warrant it or when several owners put their bucks together they are run in bands, but they are always kept separate from the ewes and lambs.

DUTIES OF HERDERS AND PACKERS.

It is the duty of the packer, who is often also the owner, to find new grazing places as fast as the feed is eaten off by the sheep, to move camp to these spots, and to keep the herder, or herders (one man sometimes packing for two bands), and himself supplied with provisions. A saddle horse and two pack horses are commonly used by the packer.

The herder's duty is to keep his band on good feed, keep the sheep in one body, bring back those that have strayed away, look out for the appearance of disease and apply the necessary remedies, and join the packer in the cooking and other camp work. If the sheep are to graze 2 or 3 miles from camp (about the maximum distance) and in the forest, they are often driven away as early as sunrise: but if the grazing is nearer camp, and especially if it is on open meadow land, the sheep seldom start out before the dew is off the grass. They graze a few hours, lie down during the middle of the day, graze again, and finally return to their bedding ground, situated usually near the camp.

The practice of herders in handling their sheep varies widely. Some are constantly with their bands, watching them closely throughout the day, carefully guiding them from one choice feeding ground to another, keeping them rounded up with a dog, and sleeping among them at night. Others leave a band to pick out their own feeding area, to take care of themselves largely, and even to select their own bedding ground, attending only in a general way to their location and seeing that the band does not divide. Sheep managed in this way are said to be better able to take care of themselves, to be less easily frightened by wild animals, to be less worried by the dogs, to trample the feed less, and to come out in quite as good condition at the end of the season. Each system doubtless has its advantages.

The bedding grounds on which the sheep "bed down," as it is called, are selected on a dry, level, or gently sloping, smooth area. At dusk the sheep come in, crowding and bleating and raising a cloud of dust. They gradually arrange themselves and one by one they lie down, close together, and little by little the bleating grows less till they all are silent and asleep.

At the end of a week, commonly, sometimes two weeks or sometimes only two or three days, the feed within easy range of camp is exhausted and the camp is moved to a new place. This moving of camp is repeated from time to time all summer, some of the bands in suitable situations remaining in one general locality, others making long circuits over a much larger territory. A particular piece of ground is usually grazed over only once, as a second grazing is seldom of any value. If, however, the first grazing is sufficiently early in the season a fresh growth may follow and furnish an excellent second crop. In general, the progress of camps during the season is from the base of the mountains toward their summits, keeping pace with the growth of the vegetation that follows the melting of the snow.

LOSS OF SHEEP DURING THE SUMMER.

From various accidental causes a few sheep in a band are usually lost during the summer, a loss of 1 per cent being common. Occasionally larger losses occur. The principal causes of death are bears, wolves, falling rocks, poisonous plants, and lightning. Grizzly bears come at night and usually kill several sheep at a visit. The only wolves of the higher mountains are the large timber wolves. They kill few sheep during the summer, but in the autumn, just about the time the sheep are leaving the mountains, they begin to run in packs and are more bold. A late band of sheep sometimes suffers a severe loss from this source. On steep, rocky mountain slopes a sheep is frequently killed by a rolling rock loosened by some sheep grazing on a higher part of the slope. Sheep are sometimes killed by eating water hemlock (*Cicuta vagans*), larkspur (*Delphinium*), rhododendron (*Rhododendron californicum*), or laurel (*Umbellularia californica*). The first two are herbaceous plants growing at low elevations on the eastern slope of the Cascades, usually below the timber. In the spring of 1897 about 200 sheep died in a band that had been grazed in a great patch of larkspur on one of the western spurs of the Tygh Hills in Wasco County. The other two plants are, respectively, a shrub and a small tree that grow on the humid western slopes in the forests. Rarely a band of sheep, driven to cover in a storm, is struck by lightning with serious results. In July, 1896, 168 sheep were killed in this way in a thunderstorm on Crane Prairie. The sheep had huddled together for shelter from the rain in a little grove of lodge-pole pines, where they were struck by two successive lightning bolts.

Formerly large losses were occasioned by the disease known as sheep scab. A State quarantine and inspection law, however, caused a decided decrease in its prevalence, and, finally, another still more powerful factor, the lowering of the price of wool resulting in a total lack of profits on scabby sheep, has now made the disease almost unknown.

STATISTICS OF SHEEP GRAZED WITHIN THE RESERVE.

One of the first pieces of information it was desired to secure was a reliable estimate of the number of sheep ranged within the reserve. The estimates secured from different sources varied so greatly, however, that they all were necessarily treated as unsatisfactory, and it was resolved to take an actual census on the ground. This was done by repeated inquiry of herders, packers, owners, and residents having a definite knowledge of the various bands. The data thus secured include the name of each owner or lessee, the number of his bands, the number of sheep in each band, the place on which they were grazing when the record was made, and the county in which the sheep were owned. The publication of all the details is unnecessary and undesirable, but a summary of the data gives the following statistics.

The total number of sheep recorded as ranging on the Cascade reserve is 188,360, contained in 86 bands, an average of 2,190 sheep per band. Classified by size the bands are as follows:

Number and size of bands on reserve.

Size of band.	Number of bands.	Size of band.	Number of bands.
a 1, 000	2	2. 300	4
1. 400	2	2. 400	3
1, 600	4	2, 500	b 22
1, 700	1	2, 700	3
1, 800	5	2, 800	1
1, 900	2	2, 900	1
2, 000	b 28	3. 000	2
2. 100	1	3, 200	1
2, 200	3	3. 500	1

a This means not less than 950 nor more than 1,049. The same relation holds for the rest of the table.

b The exceptionally large number of bands containing 2,000 and 2,500 is due to the fact that only estimates (instead of an actual count) of the number of sheep in some of the bands could be made by those from whom the information was secured, and that in making these estimates a person is much more likely to say 2,000 than 1,900 or 2,100, and 2,500 rather than 2,400 or 2,600.

Bands of less than 1,600 are usually owned by young men who are making a start in the business; bands of more than 2,700 by owners who are ranging their sheep in unusually open country, or who are injudiciously trying to save the hire of an additional herder. Of the various expenses entailed in running a band of sheep the wages of the herder and packer, the cost of their provisions, and the cost of their outfit are fixed charges, whatever the number of sheep in the band. With a small band the net profits per head are therefore less. With a larger band, the net profits per head increase until the band reaches such a size, varying with the herder and the nature of the region, that the number of strayed and lost sheep increases greatly and the others impede each other to such an extent in grazing that they produce neither a large amount nor a good quality of wool. The net profit per head then decreases, and an owner usually prefers to divide the band, purchasing enough additional sheep to make two bands of suitable size.

Classified by counties in which the sheep are owned, the statistics are as follows:

Counties in which sheep are owned.

County.	Number of bands.	Number of sheep.
Wasco	66	142,770
Crook	11	24,660
Sherman	9	20,930

Classified by the districts (described on page 21) into which the reserve may be divided for range purposes, the statistics are as follows:

Number of sheep by range districts.

Range district.	Number of bands.	Number of sheep.
Mount Hood	40	86,400
Three Sisters	36	79,330
Upper Deschutes	10	22,630

The total number of owners ranging sheep in the Cascades the past season was 60, or, more strictly speaking, there were 50 individual owners, 2 lessees, and 8 pairs of partners. It is possible that a few of those recorded as owners may in reality be lessees.

Of these 60 owners, 41 owned single bands, containing 1,000 to 3,500 sheep; 15 owned 2 bands each, containing 3,400 to 5,000 sheep; 3 owned 3 bands each, containing 5,000 to 7,980 sheep; and 1 owned 6 bands, containing 13,450 sheep.

The sheep ranges of the reserve lie in seven counties, as follows:

Location of sheep on range by counties.

County.	Number of bands.	Number of sheep.
Wasco	34	72,160
Crook	22	49,850
Klamath	1	1,600
Clackamas	6	14,240
Linn	7	13,790
Lane	14	32,220
Douglas	2	4,500

It will be observed that the sheep ranged in the Cascade reserve are chiefly in the hands of small owners; that these owners live in the counties of Wasco, Crook, and Sherman, all on the east side of the Cascade Mountains; and that of the seven counties in which the sheep are

14384—No. 15——2

grazed. three (Wasco, Crook. and Klamath) are on the east side of the Cascade crest, while four (Clackamas, Linn. Lane, and Douglas) are on the west slope.

A small percentage of the sheep grazed in the reserve, perhaps 15,000 to 20,000, are known as " Washington sheep." These are not. as might be supposed, sheep owned in the State of Washington, but sheep owned in the State of Oregon, which in earlier years were taken across the Columbia River into the Cascade Mountains of Washington for the summer. In February. 1897. the Washington State legislature passed an alleged quarantine law, stipulating a sixty-day quarantine period for all sheep entering the State. This was an effectual barrier against the sheep from Oregon, and they were compelled to find summer grazing south of the Columbia. Many of them went into the Cascade reserve, and thus for the past summer have swelled the customary total.

CHARACTER OF GRAZING LANDS.

The acreage per sheep required for grazing throughout the summer is exceedingly variable, depending on the kind and character of the vegetation. In a rich meadow, not too wet, half an acre for each sheep may be sufficient; in sterile lodgepole pine forests ten acres may be required.

To a herder the plants on which sheep graze are of three classes—grass, weeds, and browse. The name "grass" is applied not only to true grasses, but to all plants resembling grass in appearance, especially sedges and rushes. Under the head of "weeds" are included all herbaceous plants that do not have the general appearance of grasses, a difference due chiefly to their broader leaves. "Browse" is a name applied to shrubs and young trees, the leaves and twigs of which are eaten by sheep. The vegetation of the different ranges is made up of varying combinations of these three classes of forage.

As characterized by their vegetation, the summer grazing areas of the reserve may be classed under four heads—"forests," "burns," "meadows," and "balds."

The nature of the grazing in the virgin forest land varies. of course, with the character of the forests. For present purposes they may be divided into three—the yellow-pine forests, the lodgepole pine forests, and the heavy west slope forests. The distribution of these forests is a matter of climatic conditions dependent upon elevation and upon the heavy rainfall on the west slope of the Cascades and the light rainfall of the eastern slope. In general, these conditions are maintained throughout the whole length of the State, the principal exceptions occurring where in the lower gaps of the mountains the rainfall conditions of the west slope lap over upon the eastern slope.

The yellow-pine forests lie at low elevations along the eastern slope of the mountains, and constitute the first timber entered by the sheep in approaching the mountains from the plains. The principal species of tree is the yellow pine, *Pinus ponderosa*. The individual trees usually stand well apart, and there is plenty of sunshine between them. The vegetation consists of a rather poor quality of bunch grass and other scattered herbaceous plants, and a very scattered undergrowth, made up chiefly of chamise (*Kunzia tridentata*). In their upper elevations the yellow-pine forests are denser, and often contain a considerable amount of Douglas spruce (*Pseudotsuga mucronata*) and California white fir (now treated as a form of *Abies concolor*), with an undergrowth of snow brush (*Ceanothus velutinus*), manzanita (*Arctostaphylos patula*), and chinquapin (*Castanopsis chrysophylla minor*).

The lodgepole pine forests also lie chiefly on the eastern slope of the mountain, at a higher elevation than the yellow-pine forests, and present a very different character. The trees are small, thin-barked, and very easily killed by fire. The underbrush, made up chiefly of a creeping manzanita (*Arctostaphylos nevadensis*) and the waxy currant (*Ribes cereum*), is never dense, and often is entirely wanting over large areas. Grass is sparse and not of the best quality. The best grazing plants are lupines. In the lodgepole pine forests the trees are usually set close together, so close, indeed, that it is often difficult to ride through them on horseback. At a still higher elevation than the lodgepole pine, extending, indeed, almost to timber line, is the belt of black hemlock (*Tsuga pattonii*), a usually open forest with underbrush of two huckleberries (*Vaccinium scoparium* and *V. membranaceum*) or, especially at high elevations, wholly devoid of underbrush. Almost no grazing is carried on in this hemlock belt, though the bands of sheep often traverse it on their way across the mountain crests to the west slope.

The heavy west slope forests are deep, dark, and dense, and consist chiefly of a mixture of the Douglas spruce (*Pseudotsuga mucronata*) and the white fir (*Abies grandis*), with often considerable quantities of other trees. These forests bear a usually dense undergrowth and exceed in humidity both of the forests mentioned above. The grazing in the west slope forests consists chiefly of weeds and browse, the latter made up largely of vine maple (*Acer circinatum*).

The "burns" that occur in the Cascades depend largely upon the character of the forests in which they lie. For sheep-grazing purposes burns in the yellow-pine forests are of small importance one way or the other, as very little permanent change in the herbage is effected by them. The scant grass and underbrush do not make a destructive fire, while the bark of the yellow pines is so thick and so nearly devoid of resin that only under exceptional circumstances is a mature tree killed. The saplings, however, up to an age of fifteen or twenty years are readily killed by fire, and frequently an old tree well supplied with resin, exuding about some injury near the base, takes fire there year after year, gradually burning deeper and deeper, until the tree is destroyed. The scars thus made are commonly known as "fire cracks."

On rocky slopes in the higher elevations of the yellow pine forests, where there is a large admixture of white fir and Douglas spruce, and the underbrush is thicker, a forest fire is often extremely destructive to the timber, and is followed by a very dense growth of shrubs, made up chiefly of snow brush (*Ceanothus velutinus*), manzanita (*Arctostaphylos patula*), willow (*Salix nuttallii*), and chinquapin (*Castanopsis chrysophylla minor*). Sheep do not browse readily on any of these shrubs, and they frequently form thickets so dense that a band of sheep can not be driven through them. A fire in such a forest, therefore, is distinctly detrimental to the interests of sheep owners.

In the lodgepole pine forests burns are extremely common and their effect upon the timber is very pronounced. The trees have a thin bark and are easily killed without being burned up. In a few years the bare poles rot at the root just beneath the surface of the ground and are blown over by the wind, forming an inextricable tangle of small logs, sometimes extending for miles, which it is difficult for sheep to cross, and which at this stage furnish very little grazing. A second fire among these dead logs, when dry, burns them to ashes and opens the country, though it destroys whatever humus there may be upon the surface of the ground, usually only slight in these forests. After the first burning a dense growth of seedlings usually covers the ground among the dead trunks, but with the second burning these seedlings, too, are destroyed. After a few years, commonly from three to five, an area denuded by the two burnings has become covered with a growth of short sedges, often with an admixture of small vetches. The return of the pines to such an area is extremely slow, there being no old trees to seed the area thoroughly, and certain conditions, not now well understood in detail, evidently preventing chance seedlings from getting a start in the sod. These old grassy burns in the lodgepole pine forests form such a distinct type of vegetative covering that they deserve a special designation. They will be referred to in this report as "fire-glades."

The burns in the west slope forests are very destructive to timber if they occur at a dry season when the deep litter feeds the flames and everything burns readily. By the second year they are usually covered with a dense growth of weeds and browse, often interspersed with tall grasses. Within a few years, however, on account of the humidity of the climate, they grow up with underbrush, soon developing, if they are not again burned, a growth of saplings; but if repeatedly burned, supporting only a dense growth of underbrush. The exceptional conditions under which the reproduction of these forests is slow are referred to on page 36.

Natural meadows in this region are areas on which, on account of an excess of moisture, timber does not grow. The word meadow, therefore, as used in this report means always a natural wet meadow, and the name will not be applied to fire-glades nor to open dry slopes. The vegetation of meadows is in most instances made up principally of grasses and sedges. Most of the meadows in the Cascades occur at middle elevations, especially within the belt of the lodgepole pine on the eastern side of the range and the heavy west slope forest on the other side.

The "balds" are comparatively limited in extent and lie altogether, so far as observed, on the west slope of the Cascades. They consist of the dry summits of spurs and detached peaks, which, though well supplied with moisture at most seasons, are drained very rapidly when the summer drought begins, and become so dry on their summits that they will not support a forest growth. The grazing upon these summits is excellent and consists largely of what is known as mountain bunch grass (*Festuca vaseyana*).

It should be mentioned here, with reference to the different types of sheep-grazing lands above described, that the vegetation is by no means uniform over each one. Especially are local differences in vegetation due to differences in soil, and wherever the soil is made up of a very poor quality of volcanic ash, which renders the surface exceedingly dry for the greater part of the summer, underbrush, grasses, and sometimes all herbaceous vegetation may be almost entirely wanting. Areas of this description are frequent both in the lodgepole pine forests and at higher elevations in the black hemlock belt. The surprising lack of good grazing at or near timber line in the Oregon Cascades, particularly their more southerly portions, is also attributable chiefly to this cause.

LOCATION OF GRAZING AREAS.

For convenience of reference, the ranges may be divided into three districts—the Mount Hood district, the Three Sisters district, and the Upper Deschutes district. The Mount Hood district extends from the Columbia River southward to about the latitude of the northern edge of the Warm Springs Indian Reservation; the Three Sisters district from Mount Jefferson, at the southern edge of this Indian reservation, to and including the southern head waters of McKenzie River, about latitude 44° 10′; and the Upper Deschutes district from the latter line southward to and including Diamond Lake, about latitude 43° 5′. Each of these districts is subdivided into ranges, the principal ones of which may be briefly named and located as follows:

Mount Hood—White River, Gate Creek, Three Mile Creek, Badger Creek, Boulder Creek, Salmon Prairie, Zigzag Creek, Clear Lake, Clackamas Buttes, Hood River.

Three Sisters—Mount Jefferson, Three-fingered Jack, Fish Lake, Mount Washington, McKenzie River, Horse Creek, Three Sisters.

Upper Deschutes—Willamette Cow Pastures, Crane Prairie, Davis Lake, Crescent Lake, Diamond Lake.

White River: A stream rising on the southeast side of Mount Hood and flowing into the Deschutes River. The grazing along this stream lies at different elevations and includes almost every type of grazing land except balds. It is up through the watershed of White River that most of the sheep are driven which are pastured in summer south, southeast. and southwest of Mount Hood, and north of the Warm Springs Indian Reservation.

Gate Creek: One of the affluents of White River rising within the reserve but most of it lying outside of the reserve. The grazing is similar to that on White River, but the proportion of yellow-pine forest is larger.

Three Mile Creek: Same as Gate Creek.

Badger Creek: Same as Gate Creek.

Boulder Creek: Same as Gate Creek.

Salmon Prairie: A large natural meadow west of the summit of the Cascades, on the head waters of Salmon Creek. lying just south of the Oak Grove road. A claim of private ownership is pending on this land, and sheep owners who graze on it are from time to time warned off. Farther down the stream occur large burns.

Zigzag Creek: One of the affluents of Sandy River. heading on the southwest side of Mount Hood. The grazing lies at high elevations and is varied in character between dense west slope forests, burns, and small meadows.

Clear Lake: A range just east of the summit of the Cascades, on the extreme head waters of Clear Creek, which flows into the Deschutes a few miles south of White River. It was not visited by us, nor could we learn definitely the character of the grazing.

Clackamas Buttes: A range on the west side of the Cascades. near the head waters of the Clackamas River. Not visited nor described.

Hood River: A river draining the eastern slopes of Mount Hood. The range is a large one, varied in character, the best part of it lying near the northeastern corner of the Cascade reserve.

Mount Jefferson: A range on the slopes of Mount Jefferson. near the southwestern corner of the Warm Springs Reservation and on the crest of the Cascades. The grazing is chiefly in old burns and in the open forests. The Mount Jefferson range includes also a mountain a short distance to the westward, known as Minto Mountain.

Three-fingered Jack: A mountain on the crest of the Cascades, between Mount Jefferson and the Santiam-Prineville road, similar in its character to Mount Jefferson. It is commonly known simply as "Jack."

Fish Lake: A range lying near the Santiam-Prineville road, on the western slope of the Cascades and on the head waters of the Santiam and McKenzie rivers. It is varied in character, including balds, heavy west slope forests. burns, and a small amount of meadow.

Mount Washington: A range lying on the slopes of Mount Washington, between the McKenzie and Santiam roads. It is varied in character, being made up chiefly of lodge-pole pine forests, with many old burns and some meadows.

McKenzie River: A range lying in a westerly direction from the Three Sisters, on the west slope of the mountains, similar in its character to the Fish Lake range.

Horse Creek: A range lying also on the head waters of the McKenzie River, but farther to the southward than the McKenzie River range proper and in a direction southwesterly from the Three Sisters. It consists of forest-covered mountain slopes and a large area of bottom land, the latter partly open meadow and partly forest.

Three Sisters: A range lying near the crest of the Cascades, in about latitude 44° 10′, and extending chiefly down the eastern slope toward the head waters of Squaw Creek and Tumelow Creek. It is chiefly made up of natural meadows and old burns in lodgepole pine forests.

Willamette Cow Pastures: A range on the western side of the Cascades, between the southern head waters of the McKenzie and the head waters of the Willamette to the southward. It is similar in character to the Fish Lake range.

Crane Prairie: A large natural meadow or series of meadows on the head waters of the main branch of the Deschutes. This is sometimes known on the maps as the West Fork, but more commonly known in the region as the Big Deschutes, or simply Big River. Crane Prairie is the principal source of this river. Early in the season Crane Prairie is too wet for the pasturage of sheep, and in an occasional season sheep can hardly get on it at all.

Davis Lake: Like the following, one of the reservoir sources of the Deschutes. It lies on the line between the counties of Klamath and Crook. The range consists chiefly of meadows lying along the west side of the lake. Early in the season, and sometimes in very wet years throughout the season, the grazing land is so wet that sheep can not be driven upon it.

Crescent Lake: A lake lying about 10 miles southwest of Davis Lake. The range consists mostly of meadows lying to the northeast of the lake, the best known being the one called Sanderson meadows.

Diamond Lake: A body of water lying immediately west of the summit of the Cascades at the western foot of Mount Thielson and one of the sources of the Umpqua River. It is about 15 miles in a direct line north of Crater Lake. The range consists in part of meadow land at the south end of the lake, but chiefly, as on the east side of the lake and on the lower slopes of Mount Thielson, of burns.

Each of the ranges above described is divided into smaller ranges, the names of which it seems unnecessary to detail here, as they are wholly local in their use and do not appear on any maps.

KINDS OF SHEEP FORAGE.

In addition to their classification of grazing plants into three kinds—grass, weeds, and browse—the herders make one important distinction in the quality of feed. It is "light" feed, fattening quickly, but producing a "soft" fat, which is easily lost again if the sheep are compelled to travel long distances; or it is "strong" feed, not fattening so rapidly, but producing a "hard" fat, with which sheep may be driven long distances without losing much in weight. A good packer or herder, where feed is plenty, selects the feeding grounds with these conditions in view, and always puts his sheep in condition for long drives, usually giving them light feed in the early part of the summer and hardening them toward the close of the season. In general, weeds and swamp grasses are light feed, while the dry-ground bunch grasses, chamise, and acorns are strong feed. Light feed is more abundant in spring, strong feed in the autumn. Light feed is made up chiefly of succulent vegetation containing a preponderance of freshly developed nitrogenous matter; strong feed, of vegetation containing a preponderance of substances, particularly starch and other carbohydrates, fully elaborated for storage purposes in the plant. Light feed is comparable with green fodder, strong feed with grain.

Sheep when driven by hunger will eat almost any green or even dead vegetation, but it is rarely that they reach such a condition in the Cascade reserve. As a rule, they are discriminating in their choice of forage from the vegetation over which they range. The following are the plants to which, from their abundance or general suitability, attention was more particularly drawn:

Bear grass (*Xerophyllum tenax*).—The young stems and even the seed pods of this plant are readily eaten by sheep, but the tough leaves are seldom touched, and their rough margins make the mouths of the sheep sore. It was not seen south of Mount Washington.

Bluejoint grass (*Calamagrostis inexpansa cuprea*[1]).—This is one of the principal grazing plants for sheep in Salmon Prairie. It grows frequently in other similar situations.

Butterweed (*Senecio triangularis*).—An abundant plant in meadows and along streams. Sheep are very fond of it.

Clover (*Trifolium longipes*).—A favorite forage plant of sheep in and about the meadows. Several other species of clover occur.

Dwarf birch (*Betula glandulosa*).—Sheep browse upon this shrub as high as they can reach, often when the plants are small eating them to the ground, and sometimes killing them. It grows in meadows at middle elevations.

False hellebore (*Veratrum viride*).—This, popularly known as "wild Indian corn," is a plant of which sheep are extremely fond, particularly in spring, when the young shoots and leaves first appear. The roots of this plant are poisonous, but no cases of poisoning from this source were met with. It is usually found in the meadows.

Fireweed (*Chamaenerion angustifolium*).—A common plant in burns, both in the west-slope forests and the lodgepole pine forests of the eastern slopes. When young, it is a favorite food of sheep.

Huckleberry (*Vaccinium membranaceum*).—Sheep browse readily on the leaves and twigs of this kind of huckleberry, one of the tallest and most abundant species. It is very abundant on the south slope of Mount Hood and in the various other localities frequented by huckle-

[1] The grasses have been identified by Professor F. Lamson-Scribner.

berry pickers. It is a characteristic shrub of somewhat open slopes and burns in the heavy west-slope forests.

Lungwort (*Mertensia sibirica*).—This is a plant of wet situations in the west-slope forests and is readily cropped by the sheep.

Lupine or ten-finger (*Lupinus rivularis*).—This and other species of Lupinus are eagerly eaten by sheep. *Lupinus laxiflorus* is the one most widely distributed. In some parts of the lodgepole pine forest it is abundant and an important sheep forage.

Mountain bunch grass (*Festuca rascyana*).—This is considered by sheep men the best of all the forage plants in the Cascade Mountains. It is confined, so far as observed by us, to the balds west of the main crest.

Oak (*Quercus garryana*).—When the sheep are driven out of the mountains in the autumn in the Mount Hood grazing district, they pass through a belt of this oak, which grows mingled with the yellow pines at their lower elevations and along the streams at a still lower altitude. The trees are then shedding their acorns, which are commonly produced in great abundance. The sheep are extremely fond of these acorns and they often gorge themselves with them.

Pea vine (*Lathyrus*).—Various species of this genus occur throughout the Cascades, and almost all of them are readily eaten by sheep and are excellent fatteners. *Lathyrus oregonensis* is abundant in fire glades of the lodgepole pine forests.

Pine grass (*Carex pennsylvanica*).—This is the most abundant and characteristic plant of the fire-glades in the lodgepole pine forests, under suitable conditions, as at the southern end of Diamond Lake, forming a fairly dense turf. It is not considered a superior forage plant for sheep, though when it first shoots up in the spring they readily eat it. When the burned area of lodgepole pine is upon a sandy soil, the plant is more scattered, and together with a small Stipa is known as "sand feed." Sheep scatter widely upon it, and can with difficulty be held together, doubtless searching for more palatable food. From the fact that this sedge often grows, thinly, in the lodgepole pine forests it is often known as pine grass, a name applied also to various other slender grasses that grow in the same situation.

Rose (*Rosa gymnocarpa*).—This is one of the favorite browsing plants for sheep in the heavy west slope forests.

Sedge (*Carex*).—The larger part of the so-called grasses of which the meadows are made up, consists of various species of this genus. Many of them are eaten readily by sheep.

Sunflower (*Balsamorhiza deltoidea*).—A characteristic plant of the yellow-pine forests, said to be an excellent sheep food.

Sunflower (*Wyethia*).—A plant abundant toward the northern end of the Cascades in the lower elevations of the yellow-pine belt, particularly in treeless openings. It is a favorite spring food of sheep.

Three-leaf or deer-tongue (*Achlys triphylla*).—One of the character-

26

istic plants of the heavy west-slope forests and a favorite food plant of the sheep.

Valerian (*Valeriana sitchensis*).—A common plant of moist open slopes and burns in the west-slope forests, closely eaten by sheep.

Vancouveria (*Vancouveria hexandra*).—A herbaceous plant of the heavy west-slope forests, very much liked by sheep, and, so far as could be learned, not distinguished by a popular name.

Vine maple (*Acer circinatum*).—This is one of the favorite browsing shrubs of sheep, and grows in abundance in the heavy west-slope forests. We did not meet with it south of the Mount Hood range district.

Wild cat grass (*Stipa*).—This is one of the characteristic grasses of fire-glades in the lodgepole pine forests. Sheep graze upon it, but it is not considered good feed.

Wild cheat (*Bromus breviaristatus*.)—A favorite grass common in burns in the heavy west-slope forests.

Wild tansy (*Achillea millefolium*).—A favorite feed of sheep, found in a great variety of situations, usually in open ground. It is very eagerly sought after by the sheep in spring, but later in the season it becomes dry and less palatable.

Willow (*Salix*).—Many species of willow grow in the Cascades and the leaves and twigs of most of them are eaten rather readily by sheep. *Salix nuttallii* is a characteristic species of burns in the heavy west-slope forests. The others grow chiefly in meadows and along streams.

Wire grass (*Juncus balticus*).—This plant, which grows in meadows, is eaten by sheep, but not with much relish.

EFFECTS OF OVERGRAZING.

The effect of a moderate amount of grazing on the lands of the reserve is the same as the effect of the judicious removal of a grass crop from a fenced pasture by grazing or from a meadow by cutting; namely, that a forage crop is secured without material detriment to the land and the herbaceous vegetation it bears. The expression "a moderate amount of grazing" is used advisedly; for there is not the slightest question that in many countries of the Old World and in some localities of the United States overgrazing is a serious injury to the forage crop and to the young growth of forests. By "a moderate amount of grazing" is meant grazing only to such an extent that the forage crop does not decrease from year to year. In general, overgrazing in the Cascades has only been begun, or perhaps the facts are better expressed by the statement that up to the present time overgrazing is limited to a few areas in a part of the Mount Hood district and a part of the Three Sisters district. For example, a small range on the west slope of the Cascades near Mount Washington, containing an area of about a section, formerly maintained a band of sheep eight weeks, but now can support them only about half as long. Overgrazing on a very small scale can be seen almost anywhere in a sheep country, on bedding grounds and along well-worn routes of travel for sheep. In such situations are commonly seen the primary bad effects of overgrazing; namely, the weakening or killing not only of the herbaceous vegetation, but of shrubs, seedling trees, and the smaller saplings.

The principal bad effects of overgrazing are to be attributed rather to trampling than to actual close cropping. There are very few plants which from simply being eaten off will fail to grow again, but where repeatedly trampled, particularly in wet weather, when the plants are soft and the roots are easily pressed out of the ground, almost any plant will suffer. Two bad effects are observable from this abuse, (1) the washing of the soil and (2) the killing of the vegetation, followed by the substitution of other less valuable forage plants.

Almost the whole territory contained in the Cascade forest reserve is made up of a rather loose soil of volcanic origin. It does not wash and gully very seriously even when exposed to the action of water. Up to this time the damage in the mountains due to this cause has amounted practically to nothing in any of the localities visited by us.

The killing of the natural vegetation through trampling and overgrazing has only barely been begun; and the result which is always to be expected, namely, the substitution of useless weeds for the original vegetation, has not yet occurred. The principal evidence of overgrazing thus far is in the decrease of the amount of pasturage afforded by particular ranges. As cited above, a portion of the Mount Washington range, known as Bunch Grass Ridge, originally maintained a band of sheep eight weeks, but it now keeps a band only about half as long. The same may be said of a large portion of the range that lies immediately to the east of the Three Sisters, an area which is crossed by many bands of sheep in going to and from the western part of the Three Sisters range district.

While overgrazing in the mountains has not reached the point of extensively damaging the range, in many portions of the plains to the east of the mountains the opposite is true. Along Hay Creek, for example, are gullies 20 feet deep in the hard adobe or gumbo soil which have been washed out by the water pouring down from the adjacent hills long since denuded of grass by overgrazing. This washing has taken place since the region was settled and principally within the last fifteen years. The actual substitution of useless introduced weeds for the valuable native forage plants may be seen on a large scale on the Tygh Hills north of Tygh Valley and west of the Deschutes River, a substitution which under present conditions is bound to continue.

One of the first evidences of overgrazing in the mountains is the restlessness of sheep herders, who, finding a customary range becoming short, drive their bands to some other range, which they expect to find in better condition. Disappointed, they drive on to still another range, and so the bands follow each other about, wearing out their sheep by overdriving, and leaving the range with their stock in a very exhausted condition.

Over most of the reserve the actual damage to the young growth of timber is up to the present time confined chiefly to small areas, such as bedding grounds and routes of travel. In such situations the young pines, low enough to be reached and nibbled by the sheep, may be seen standing crooked and incapable of developing into sound trees of a healthy growth, while seedlings are trampled out entirely. The trouble from this source, however, is constantly misunderstood on both sides. I passed through an area of forest land on McKay Mountain, a western spur of the Blue Mountains lying in a direction northeast from Prineville, where sheep had been grazed for twenty-five years. This is the oldest sheep range in Crook County. In these forests were frequent areas of young saplings of thoroughly healthy and symmetrical form which unquestionably had not received the slightest injury from sheep grazing. At the same time along the road were seen frequently the gnarled and stunted pine saplings, which showed clearly what doubtless occurred over wider areas where overgrazing and trampling were similarly carried to an extreme.

The forest conditions on this Blue Mountain spur might form the text for a long discussion on the effects of forest grazing, but there is room here for only a brief comment on a phase of the question that is likely to escape popular notice. Under ordinary conditions when an opening is made in a forest by the death and fall of an old tree, and more sunlight comes down to the ground, a dense growth of saplings springs up to fill the opening. The saplings, competing with each other for the light, send up straight, tall trunks, and the one or two trees that finally excel the others and fill the opening possess tall, limbless trunks, which make the best of saw logs. If for any reason the seedlings in such an opening are injured so that only a few live and develop into saplings they grow into limb-covered trees, valueless for lumber. In this Blue Mountain spur the effect of sheep grazing will be seen in the next generation of timber. On those areas in which for any reason the sheep have not killed the seedlings a good quality of timber can be cut, while those areas on which most of the seedlings are now being tramped out every year will bear trees but not lumber.

FOREST FIRES IN THE CASCADE RESERVE.

Whatever may be the amount of damage due thus far to overgrazing, the popular mind has associated with the forest grazing of sheep, if not distinctly as an effect, certainly as a necessary accompaniment, a kind of forest damage immeasurably more disastrous up to the present time than overgrazing, and now almost universally recognized as a public calamity, namely, forest fires. Without reference to the truth or falsity of this popular belief regarding the cause of forest fires in sheep-grazing districts, the subject is one of such far-reaching effect on the welfare of a State and the communities of which it is made up, that to ascertain the causes of forest fires and to devise means for their prevention are pressing and fundamental necessities. As already stated, in our investigation the reserve was traversed from the southern to the northern end. I am confident that there does not exist in the whole reserve a township of forest land in some part of which forest fires have not occurred, and it was difficult to find even a single square mile in which the evidences of fire, recent or remote, were not present. We contemplated an estimate of the acreage of burned areas, but this plan for several reasons was necessarily abandoned. It is possible, therefore, to make only the general but no less positive statement that in addition to areas burned over with comparatively little damage to the commercial timber, the reserve contains hundreds of thousands of acres on which the timber has been wholly destroyed by fire.

Especial attention was paid in our field examination to the subject of forest fires. Whenever possible we ascended the highest peaks and from them examined the adjacent country for the purpose of ascertaining the location of forest fires. In this way we saw about 40 fires in various parts of the reserve, some of them large, most of them small. The effect of fires upon different types of timber has already been described. (See pages 19 and 20.)

In connection with the relation of forest fires to sheep grazing it was necessary to examine with the greatest care into the causes of forest fires.

EARLY FOREST FIRES.

Historically considered, we must look to the Indians as the first manipulators of forest fires in this region. It is a clearly established fact, based on observation, that the Indians of the Willamette Valley in western Oregon were accustomed before the advent of white men in that region, to as late a period as the early forties, to set fire to the grass for the purpose of burning it off. Their object in doing this is supposed to have been chiefly (1) to cause a fresh growth of grass in the autumn, upon which enormous quantities of wild fowl descended to feed, particularly geese, and (2) for the purpose of killing and roasting .for food the great quantities of grasshoppers that in certain years fed upon the grass. Similar uses of fire by the aborigines in other parts of the western United States have been recorded by which they were enabled to keep certain large areas denuded of timber. Upon the cessation of these fires, by reason of the intervention of white settlers, the timber has begun again to encroach upon such areas, and in the Willamette Valley, for example, we now see frequent groves of Douglas spruce (*Pseudotsuga mucronata*) and white fir (*Abies grandis*) about fifty years of age, of remarkably uniform and symmetrical growth, which have developed through their natural seeding without human assistance.

Just how many of the old burns in the Cascade reserve are to be attributed to the Indians it is impossible to say, but several fire-glades were seen which must have antedated by several decades the settlement of the country by whites, fire-glades in which the evidence of fire was confined to pieces of charred wood that lay beneath the surface of the ground, hardly showing the lines of the long-since rotten, logs to which they belonged. Such fire-glades occur on the ridges south of Huckleberry Mountain, southwest of Crater Lake, which is well known to have been a favorite resort of the aborigines for many generations. In general, however, the number of fires of sufficient age to be attributable to this period is small. The Indians probably can not be accused of starting fires to a large extent accidentally, or of setting fires indiscriminately, but it is undoubtedly true that at certain seasons it was their custom to set fires in the mountains intentionally and systematically, in connection with their fall hunting excursions, when deer were driven together and killed in large numbers.

A second great source of fires in the Cascades was the early road building across the mountains to connect eastern with western Oregon. A broad band of fires usually accompanied such an enterprise. At that time the amount of destruction thus caused was not appreciated, because most of those who were connected with the building of these roads were from the Eastern States, where timber was abundant and where the first prerequisite of agricultural progress was to burn off timber in order to clear the land for farming purposes. The details of an interesting method of felling large trees of Douglas spruce (*Pseudotsuga mucronata*) were learned from some of the old inhabitants. The trees are large, commonly 6 feet in diameter at maturity, and to cut them was too expensive and difficult a task. The method of felling the tree was to bore a hole with a long auger diagonally downward to the heart of the tree and to bore another similar hole diagonally upward from the base of the tree, connecting with the first. A live coal was then dropped into the hole, and the draft through the two auger holes causing the wood to take fire, a roaring conflagration followed which burned away a large portion of the tree trunk. It was seldom that an axe had to be used to fell the tree, as the fire almost always ate away a sufficient portion of the trunk to cause it to fall.

These early causes of fires, however, are now matters of history and need to be taken into consideration at the present time only in so far as they explain the origin of many of the old well-known burns that antedate the era of sheep grazing in the Cascades.

RECENT FIRES IN THE RANGES AND THEIR CAUSES.

Of the fires of the present period it may be said in the first place that they are by no means confined to the sheep-grazing areas. Parts of the southern Cascades in which sheep have never been grazed were found to be riddled with fires, and in general it may be stated that forest fires in this region increase proportionately to the increase of human occupancy, whether the occupants are sheep herders, campers, road builders, prospectors, or any other class of men.

Travelers, campers, and Indians.—It will be of interest to give a somewhat detailed account of the causes of the fires observed by our party in the course of its travels through the mountains. The greatest number of fires should be attributed to the class of people known as "travelers," families without a definite place of residence, usually illiterate and poor, who journey about in covered wagons from one State to another or from one portion of a State to another, grazing their horses on the public lands and occasionally by an odd job earning a little money with which to buy provisions. Repeatedly camp fires were seen which had been left by these people and which under suitable conditions might have caused disastrous forest fires. At the time of year when the forest litter and the underbrush are dry a strong wind suddenly springing up very frequently causes one of these abandoned camp fires to develop into a highly destructive agency.

It is clear that a very large majority of the fires in the Cascade forests are due to carelessness rather than to maliciousness, and the efforts of the Interior Department must undoubtedly be chiefly directed rather toward preventing carelessness in handling fires than toward the detection of malicious fire setters. From the people who showed a willingness to give information as to the causes of fires it was extremely rare to learn of a case in which a fire had been known to be set maliciously, though fires known to have been due to carelessness were matters of every-day comment.

Camping parties, particularly those made up of young and inexperienced people from towns, are a fertile source of forest fires. These parties commonly go into the woods for a summer outing, often making the chief object of their pleasure the hunting and fishing afforded by the region. Some of these parties are made up of young men who go into the woods for the special purpose of hunting, but who have little experience in woodcraft and no knowledge of the proper method of handling a camp fire. They are often referred to as hunters, but it is known that real hunters of experience and that old campers of experience are extremely careful in these matters. Perhaps the designation "alleged hunters" applied to them by an old rancher and woodsman of eastern Oregon will sufficiently distinguish them from real hunters.

The Indians from the two Indian reservations at the east base of the mountains, the Klamath Reservation and the Warm Springs Reservation, still go into the mountains in the autumn to pick huckleberries and to hunt. Information was given of the most diametrically opposite character regarding these Indians with reference to forest fires, it being stated by some that the Indians were invariably careful to put out a fire before leaving, by others that they set fires indiscriminately. There was little opportunity to learn definitely how many fires should be attributed to this source, but the writer saw a brightly burning fire at a recently abandoned camp of Warm Springs Indians on Salmon Prairie. The day was rainy, however, and it is possible that under other conditions they would have extinguished the fire before leaving the camp. It would be a wise precaution for the Indian agents to see that when they issue permits to the Indians to go off the reserve it should be distinctly with the understanding that they are to set no forest fires, and that they are to be held strictly responsible if they transgress this regulation.

Road improvement.—On August 4, while traveling on the west slope of the Rogue River-Fort Klamath road, the writer and party passed, between White Horse Creek and the Crater Lake fork of the road, a distance of about 3 miles, six fires that had evidently been set to burn stumps or fallen dead trees out of the road. One of these fires was burning close to standing timber, had already destroyed several logs upon the ground, and was roaring through the top of a small black hemlock. It might very easily have been carried into a large area of standing timber, and had a strong wind sprung up no one could have prevented this result. Not far above this place a man was seen with a two-horse wagon and tools, who was engaged in improving the same stretch of road. He had been prying small logs out of the road with a crowbar, cutting off obstructing tree roots with an ax, and shoveling soil into the holes in the road. It was unquestionably this man, doubtless the road supervisor of the district or someone employed by him, who had set the fires. In reply to a question the man, stopping work on the log he was engaged upon, said: "Oh, I am going to pick this one to pieces and burn it out after a while." Whether any of these fires afterwards developed into large forest fires there is no means of knowing, but a fire set for the same purpose along the road near the northwestern corner of Klamath Lake had become unmanageable and burned over a considerable area. When the party passed the place the fire had been extinguished, and only the destruction caused by it was seen. Regarding this possible source of forest fires, especially with a knowledge of the very disastrous forest fires due to the early road builders, it should be said that officers in charge of such work, if they must employ this means of clearing the road, should watch the fires closely, and should invariably see that they are finally extinguished.

Lightning.—It has often been claimed that many forest fires are due to lightning. Little credence was at first given to this. Many men were found who had heard of fires that originated in this way, but only rarely a man who had ever seen one. One day as Mr. Applegate and the writer were upon a peak at the junction of the Calapooia Mountains with the Cascades, looking for forest fires, we saw not more than half a a mile away in the forest a small fire, considerably larger, however, than a camp fire should have been. The region was one remote from the ordinary routes of travel or any place of public resort. We were therefore curious to know how the fire had been started, supposing it had been caused by a wandering hunter. Upon going to the fire and making an examination we were astonished to find no evidence of a camp and were puzzled, until Mr. Applegate cried: "Look at that tree!" The tree was a handsome live Shasta fir, which had very recently been struck by lightning. The tree was still standing, but pieces of bark and shattered wood had been thrown in all directions through the woods to a distance of at least 200 feet. The tree was exactly 10 feet in circumference. The fire had been confined to the ground, and had burned over a small area about 50 by 200 feet, including eleven large trees of black hemlock and amabilis fir, several fallen dead trees, and probably two hundred saplings, most of them small ones. The forest litter and some of the logs were still burning, but on account of the presence of many green saplings in the undergrowth and of a small huckleberry (*Vaccinium scoparium*) the fire was progressing slowly. Indeed, the forest litter was so light that only a very strong wind could have made the fire a destructive one. In other situations, or under slightly different circumstances, however, the fire might have proved very disastrous. Not long afterwards, near the northeast base of Mount Washington, the party passed through a thunderstorm of an extremely violent character, in which the strokes were repeated and terrific, and many trees in the immediate neighborhood must have been struck. The rainfall accompanying this storm, though evidently sufficient to put out any fire that may have arisen, was much lighter than the writer has ever seen in the eastern United States, and he was informed that sometimes not enough rain accompanies such a storm to dampen the forest litter. It is possible that lightning fires may be much more frequent in the Cascades than has been supposed, and the subject is certainly one worthy of further investigation.

Other causes.—Near the head of Wood River, on some mountains to the east of the reserve in the Fort Klamath country, occurred in early August a destructive forest fire. It was impossible to examine this fire on the spot, but persons who had looked into the matter with care stated that the fire had originated in a camp of some men who were splitting shakes, a sort of large, coarse shingle. The men had set a number of small fires to keep themselves, so they said, from annoyance by mosquitoes. This fire is estimated to have burned over 15,000 to 18,000 acres.

A few instances are known of small forest fires starting from smudges which had been set in a pile of rotten logs to protect camp horses from mosquitoes and other insects.

Alleged hunters, in the belief that deer will hunt out smoke to rid themselves of deer flies, are said to set single fires and sometimes lines of fires in the woods, particularly in the vicinity of salt licks. There is good reason to believe that fires of this character frequently occur. In August of this year a fire was burning in the vicinity of a salt lick in Anna Creek Canyon, in a locality away from the route of travel and

34

of such inaccessibility that only a man searching for game is likely to have been there. It is very probable that this fire was set for such a purpose.

RELATION OF FIRES TO SHEEP GRAZING.

It is of primary importance in this investigation that an unbiased opinion should be given on the relation borne by sheep herders to forest fires. It has been alleged that sheep herders systematically set fire to the forest in order to burn off the timber so that a growth of weeds and grass will spring up to furnish grazing in succeeding years. On the other hand the publication of this statement within the past year in Oregon newspapers has brought forth most positive denials by stockmen that this practice exists. This phase of the subject was a matter of special inquiry. All classes of people were asked again and again about this matter, and whenever a man stated that such a practice exists an endeavor was made to find out the place, the time, and all other detailed circumstances of the cases with which he was familiar. But it was always difficult upon asking such details to secure anything more than inconclusive circumstantial evidence. From the people who were antagonistic to sheep grazing in the Cascades it would have been possible to learn of very few cases positively attributable to this cause. With the sheepmen themselves, however, we talked very frankly, and as a result of these conversations it may be stated, without betraying any confidences and without citing individual cases, as unquestionably true that in the early days of sheep grazing in the Cascades there was a widespread belief among the sheepmen that burning off the forest was of positive benefit to the sheep-grazing industry, and that many herders undoubtedly did systematically burn over areas in the forest, either where the density of the timber had prevented the growth of suitable grazing plants, or where they had already grazed and were about to remove to another camp, or when they were leaving the forest at the end of the season. How general this practice was it is impossible to say. Many of the sheep herders and packers deny ever having set fires themselves or ever having known of a fire being set by others. No doubt in many cases such claims are correct.

It is clear that at the present time most sheep herders and packers are extremely careful not to allow their camp fires to spread and not to set fires intentionally. This is attributable to various causes. In the first place, the increase in the West of a knowledge of the importance of protecting the national timber resources has been very marked, and rarely is a man found who is not ready to say that in his opinion the Western forests should be preserved from fire. Governor Lord has urged upon the State legislature the importance of preserving the forests within the State. The following quotation is from his biennial message as published in the Portland Oregonian for March 31, 1897:

The frequent destruction of our forests by fires, caused by carelessness or design, should be stopped. Their preservation is a matter of great importance, and if something is not done to prevent it great injury will result to our timber interests. This is a subject that demands your attention, and some means must be devised for better enforcement of our laws.

The State of Oregon has passed a stringent fire law, the United States Government has passed a still more stringent fire law,[1] and although no criminal convictions have as yet been made under these acts, a knowledge that they would be made on sufficient evidence has been a strong factor in preventing fires from being set openly. Some notices of these laws have been posted at camping places through the forests, but not by any means to such an extent as is desirable. It is undoubtedly true, also, that the popular accusation of sheepmen as fire setters has acted as an effective warning to them. They realize that unless the reasons for this accusation are removed there is a strong probability of their exclusion from the reserve, and this has led them both to be more careful with fires and to insist publicly that they are careful.

The necessity of forest fires to the summer grazing industry has undoubtedly been overestimated both by the general public and frequently by stockmen themselves. A fire on an occupied range is objectionable, because it both burns up the forage and menaces the sheep herder's camp, and often the sheep themselves. Cases are known in which a whole camp outfit and provisions have been burned by the accidental spreading of a fire while a herder was away from camp with his sheep, and other cases are known in which sheep have narrowly missed being caught and burned up in a forest fire. Besides this a single fire in the black-pine belt, for example, is followed after a few years by such a growth of saplings among fallen logs as to make it exceedingly difficult to drive a band of sheep through. If the logs are charred, the wool of the sheep becomes blackened by the charcoal dust to such an extent as to decrease the value of the wool often a cent a pound. Furthermore, as already stated under the head of the effect of fires in the upper portion of the yellow-pine belt, a fire is often followed by a dense growth of underbrush, which in itself prevents a growth of forage and makes traveling across such an area almost impossible.

Against these statements, however, may be set the indisputable fact that a large amount of the grazing in the Cascades is upon old burns and that had these fires never occurred the available grazing area would have been reduced by precisely that amount.

The statement is often heard among sheep herders that close grazing is a positive benefit to the forests, because it prevents the spread of forest fires by the removal of the leaves and branches that later make up the dry forest litter. That the forests may be kept clean in this manner is unquestionable, but it is equally unquestionable that this means of preventing forest fires would prove very costly in the end. This has already been discussed under the head of overgrazing.

---

[1] For the full text of these laws, see pages 37 and 38.

The party did not come upon any fires that could be traced to sheep herders or packers, nor did we learn of any fires known to have been set by them, but we did see fires in localities where sheep had been grazed, and some of them doubtless originated from this source, probably having spread by accident, possibly by intent. It is clear that the extent of the practice among sheepmen of systematically setting forest fires has been overestimated. It is interesting to note that during the progress of the season's investigation, while no fires were found that could be traced by positive evidence to sheepmen, camp fires were seen abandoned by travelers, by campers, and by Indians, fires set by road builders and by lightning, and fires set for the purpose of creating smudges.

SLOWNESS OF REFORESTATION UNDER ADVERSE CONDITIONS.

One phase of the forest fire evil in the Cascades must still be mentioned, the slowness of reforestation in certain areas. On several of the old burns there was evidence that many years had elapsed since the fires that destroyed the trees had done their work, and upon inquiry it was found that a surprisingly long period had intervened. It was stated, for example, that the burn on the upper west slope of the Santiam-Prineville road occurred earlier than thirty years ago. This burn is now grown up to snowbrush (*Ceanothus relutinus*) and other shrubs, and no evidences of reforestation are in sight. Some portions of the great burn on the south slope of Mount Hood, we were informed, are more than forty years old and at present they bear only scattered saplings. It is clear that in many such areas, where the conditions are naturally unfavorable to the growth of trees, reforestation must be extremely slow, and a hundred years is not too low an estimate for the period that must elapse before a young forest covering of even moderate density will return.

MEANS OF LESSENING FIRES.

Before leaving this subject it is desirable to make certain suggestions which, from experience, it is believed will prove useful, in addition to the more special provisions outlined below, in reducing the number of forest fires. Have printed upon cloth, and with suitable catch words for headings, in conspicuous type, notices of the forest-fire laws and their penalties, pointing out especially that not merely is the setting of forest fires punishable by fine and imprisonment, but that leaving a camp fire without extinguishing it is also punishable in the same manner. These notices should be posted at frequent intervals along all the roads that enter or cross the reserve and at as many camping places as possible. The number of fire notices now in the Cascade forest reserve is altogether too small, and some of them being printed on paper and in an inconspicuous manner are easily overlooked or destroyed by the elements. There should be twenty notices where there is now but one. Scores of postmasters and other Government employees or persons interested in the preservation of the forests would take pleasure in posting these notices at suitable places.

One or a few convictions under the general forest-fire law of the United States would prove of the highest importance as a warning and a check to carelessness. The malicious fire setter usually so covers up his tracks that it is difficult to secure evidence sufficient to convict, but a conviction for the minor offense of leaving a camp fire without extinguishing it would be extremely easy. Our party, had that been our business, could readily have secured in several cases evidence sufficient to convict of this offense.

FIRE LAWS.

In order to call more directly to the attention of those who shall receive this report the seriousness of the offense of setting forest fires, the Oregon fire law and the Federal forest-fire law are cited in full.

OREGON FIRE LAW.

AN ACT to protect timber and other property from fire.

Be it enacted by the legislative assembly of the State of Oregon:

SECTION 1. If any person shall maliciously, with intent to injure any other person, by himself or any other person, kindle a fire on his own land or the land of any other person, and by means of such fire the buildings, fences, crops, or other personal property, or wooded timber lands of any other person shall be destroyed or injured, he shall, on conviction, be punished by a fine not less than twenty dollars nor more than one thousand dollars, or by imprisonment in the county jail not less than three months nor more than twelve months, according to the aggravation of the offense.

SEC. 2. If any person shall without malice kindle any fire in any field, pasture, enclosure, forest, prairie, or timber land not his own, without the consent of the owner, and the same shall spread and do damage to any building, fences, crops, cord wood, bark, or other personal property not his own, or to any wood or timber land not his own, he shall, on conviction, be punished by a fine of not less than ten dollars nor more than one hundred dollars and costs, according to the aggravation of the offense, and shall stand committed until the fine and costs are paid.

SEC. 3. Any person who shall enter upon the lands of another person for the purpose of hunting or fishing, and shall, without the consent of the owner of said lands, kindle any fire thereon, shall be punished by a fine of not less than ten dollars nor more than one hundred dollars; and if such fire is kindled maliciously, and with the intent to injure any other person, such offender shall be punished by a fine not less than twenty dollars nor more than two hundred and fifty dollars, or by imprisonment in the county jail not less than three months nor more than twelve months.

SEC. 4. Any person or persons who shall wilfully set fire to any wooded country or forest belonging to the State or to the United States, or to any person or persons, shall be deemed guilty of a misdemeanor, and upon conviction before a court of competent jurisdiction, shall be punished by a fine not exceeding one thousand dollars, or imprisonment not exceeding one year, or by both such fine and imprisonment: *Provided*, That nothing herein contained shall apply to any person who in good faith sets a back-fire to prevent the extension of a fire already burning.

SEC. 5. Upon any prosecution under this act, one-half of the fine imposed shall be paid to the person who first gives information thereof to the district attorney for the district in which the offense is committed, and the other moiety shall be paid into the county treasury for the benefit of the common-school fund of the county in which said fine is collected.

SEC. 6. It is hereby made the duty of the governor of this State to issue a proclamation on the first day of July of each year, calling public attention to the provisions of this act and warning all persons against violating the same. It is also made the duty of each circuit judge of this State to read the provisions of this act to each grand jury when charging them as to their duties.

SEC. 7. Inasmuch as there is urgent necessity for the protection of timber and other property from fires, this bill shall take effect and be enforced from and after its approval by the governor.

Filed in the office of the secretary of state, February 20, 1893.

FEDERAL FOREST-FIRE LAW.

AN ACT to prevent forest fires on the public domain

Be it enacted by the Senate and House of Representatives of the United States of America in Congress assembled, That any person who shall willfully or maliciously set on fire, or cause to be set on fire, any timber, underbrush, or grass upon the public domain, or shall carelessly or negligently leave or suffer fire to burn unattended near any timber or other inflammable material, shall be deemed guilty of a misdemeanor, and, upon conviction thereof in any district court of the United States having jurisdiction of the same, shall be fined in a sum not more than five thousand dollars, or be imprisoned for a term of not more than two years, or both.

SEC. 2. That any person who shall build a camp fire, or other fire, in or near any forest, timber, or other inflammable material upon the public domain, shall, before breaking camp or leaving said fire, totally extinguish the same. Any person failing to do so shall be deemed guilty of a misdemeanor, and, upon conviction thereof in any district court of the United States having jurisdiction of the same, shall be fined in a sum not more than one thousand dollars, or be imprisoned for a term of not more than one year, or both.

SEC. 3. That in all cases arising under this act the fines collected shall be paid into the public school fund of the county in which the lands where the offense was committed are situate.

Approved, February 24, 1897.

RELATION OF FOREST FIRES IN THE CASCADES TO WATER SUPPLY.

One of the cogent reasons for the preservation of our Western forests in general is the importance of a forest covering in conserving and regulating the water supply needed for irrigation purposes. An investigation of the effects of sheep grazing in the Cascade Reserve would not be complete without a consideration of this phase of the subject.

The west slope of the Cascade Range of Oregon has a heavy rainfall, and in the country through which this rainfall flows, chiefly the valleys of the Willamette. Rogue, and Umpqua rivers, irrigation is carried on only to a very small extent, and the water supply is more than sufficient. Therefore, so far as the west slope of the Cascades is concerned, the question of preserving the water supply for irrigation purposes does not arise.

The general question of the extent of the influence of forest denudation on the increase of floods is in such a state of controversy that no specific general conclusion can be drawn. We have no information relative to the west slope of the Cascades that throws any new light on the subject. The closely related subject of the washing and gullying of soil is also one with which this report has little concern. Within the reserve the damage from this source up to the present time is pracically nothing.

On the eastern slope the reserve is drained chiefly by the Deschutes River; partly, toward the south, by the tributaries of the Klamath River. The southern sources of the Deschutes and the principal sources of the Klamath River in the Cascades are in a peculiar country, geologically. The soil in this region consists chiefly of pulverized pumice stone or volcanic ashes. Neither melting snow nor rain falling upon this soil is drained off upon the surface, but sinks rapidly and appears in the form of enormous springs near the base of the mountains or upon their lower slopes. These springs are of nearly uniform flow throughout the year, and it is very questionable whether the denudation of these pumice-soil areas through forest fires or other causes would have a material effect upon their flow, and therefore upon the flow of the streams that depend upon them. These waters are comparatively little used for irrigation purposes, but assuming that they will be used to a far greater extent hereafter, it is doubtful whether special provisions for the preservation of the forest covering in this portion of the Cascades will ever prove necessary in this connection.

In other types of soil, however, such as those which exist from the Three Sisters northward—soils in which the water does not at once penetrate, but usually flows away on or near the surface—the conditions are entirely different, and while no positive and conclusive evidence can be presented that such denudation as has taken place up to the present time has caused a deficiency of irrigation water, it is clear that further denudation might readily do so. Changes might result which would be of serious detriment to the interests of the country, including all the area from Tumelow Creek northward to the Columbia. At the present time this area is only beginning its development as a grain-raising country, and whenever better methods of transportation are secured, such as are now promised by a railroad system the construction of which has already been begun, the importance of water for irrigation purposes will become constantly greater.

It was stated by Mr. W. R. Booth, keeper of the toll gate on the eastern slope of the Santiam-Prineville road, a man violently opposed to mountain sheep grazing, that many of the mountain streamlets that formerly flowed throughout the season were now drying up in summer. He cited as examples that Cache Creek carries less and less water every year, and that a streamlet four miles northwest of the toll gate, emptying into Blue Lake and finally into the Metolias, in 1893 flowed a full stream, in 1894 less, and in 1895 "went dry." It was dry in the fall of 1896 and again in 1897. Mr. O. C. Yocum, who has lived at Government Camp on the southwest slope of Mount Hood for fifteen years, stated that on areas burned within that period, streamlets that before ran all the season now become dry almost as soon as the snow has gone. These observations, if correct, indicate that denudation of these mountain slopes by forest fires may be expected to influence, perhaps seriously, the flow of their dependent streams.

IRRIGATION IN WASCO COUNTY.

Among the people of the country the only demand that has arisen for a protection of the water supply seems to be confined to a portion of Wasco County, consisting of the section between the Deschutes River on the east, the Warm Springs Indian Reservation on the south, and the Columbia River on the north. Here is a strip of territory varying from 10 to 15 miles in width, bounded on the east by the Deschutes River and on the west by the forest area of the Cascade Mountains. This strip of territory is a plateau devoid of trees and divided by east and west canyons into separate blocks. The largest of these blocks is the one lying immediately south of the canyon of White River, abutting upon the Deschutes River on the east in a canyon wall nearly 2,000 feet in height. This block is known as the Waupinitia Plain, or Juniper Flat. The principal industry of the whole strip is wheat raising. The rainfall is so limited that the wheat crop is frequently a failure, and from the peculiar situation of the plain, drained on three sides and receiving no streams from the fourth, many of the ranches during the summer drought are wholly without water. When the wells "go dry," water for household purposes and sometimes even for stock must be hauled by wagon, the ranchers in some cases being compelled to go 8 miles for it, making a round trip of 16 miles. To remedy the difficulty, irrigation ditches are now being constructed to carry water to the ranches, to be used chiefly for watering stock, for domestic purposes, and for irrigating a garden patch and a small orchard for each rancher.

Mr. Samuel B. Driver, a rancher living near Wamic, on one of the blocks of the plateau north of the Waupinitia Plain, stated that the adjacent streams—Rock Creek, Gate Creek, and Three Mile Creek—have shown a gradual decline in the last ten years in the amount of their summer flow. This decline he attributes to the trampling of the ground by sheep in the mountains at the head waters of these streams. He believes that within thirty years there will be no water in the stream beds in the fall of the year. To these statements should be offset the contrary evidence of other residents. The sheepmen in general and some of the ranchers maintained that the decline of water was wholly accounted for by the tapping of these streams with irrigating ditches. As a sheep packer tersely expressed it in the idiom of the region, "Why, the creeks can't *pack* enough water to fill the —— ditches."

Careful inquiry for actual records of summer water levels were made, but none were found. Some valuable information in this direction, however, was secured from Mr. W. M. McCorkle, of Tygh Valley, who for eighteen years has maintained a gristmill on Badger Creek, another of the streams on the head waters of which sheep are grazed in summer. Only one irrigation ditch, carrying 12 inches of water, has been taken out of this stream. About three-fourths of the water carried by the stream in summer is used by the mill. Mr. McCorkle states that this creek has had no higher nor more turbid spring floods in recent years and carries no less water in summer than formerly. This is the only information secured in the nature of a stream measurement. Certainly the mill owner would have noted any important diminution in a margin of only one-fourth.

The available evidence is not sufficient to settle this question, but the ranchers, while every opportunity for careful consideration of their proposition is due them, must present a stronger case than they have yet presented if they are to maintain their contention.

EFFECT OF FORESTS ON THE MELTING OF SNOW.

The influence of the forest cover of the Cascades on the melting of snow was a matter on which information was sought. During the winter of 1896-97 there was a controversy in the Oregon newspapers, in which Mr. John Minto maintained that the forest covering was of no value in lessening the rapidity of the melting of snow in spring. The points made by Mr. Minto were that in small groves of trees the snow goes off in spring earlier than in surrounding open areas; that the temperature inside a forest is slightly higher in winter than in the open; and that the great snow areas left upon the mountains late in summer are almost invariably outside the forest area. On these premises Mr. Minto based his conclusion.

By actual observation and by the securing of snow-fall records and other facts it was learned that while Mr. Minto's premises are of unquestioned accuracy his conclusions do not follow, and that as a matter of fact over almost the whole timbered area the snow goes off much more slowly in spring than in open areas under the same conditions. It is true, and there are various evident reasons why it should be true, that under a small grove of trees in an open plain the ground becomes bare earlier in the spring than in the open, but it is unnecessary to go into the details here. It is true from actual temperature records that the shade temperature within a forest is slightly higher than the shade temperature in the open, but this is not the only condition that affects the melting of snow. It is true in general that the snow found upon mountains late in summer lies upon open slopes; but this is due to a heavy snow-fall, dense drifting, and a retarded melting caused by low temperature at these high elevations or on northerly exposures. The absence of timber does not prevent the snow from melting, but the presence of snow through the whole or nearly the whole year has prevented the growth of timber.

In the Fort Klamath plain, part of which is timbered and part open, it was found that the snow disappeared in spring about six weeks earlier in the open than in the forest. At Government Camp, on the southwest slope of Mount Hood, we were informed, the snow lies about six weeks longer in the forest than it does on denuded areas having the same exposure and elevation. Similar information was received regarding various other areas, and the general fact that the timber covering retards the melting of snow is abundantly and conclusively shown.

FUTURE OF SHEEP GRAZING IN OREGON.

Before proceeding to a consideration of the method of dealing with the sheep-grazing question, an estimate of the future of the industry, so far as it affects the Cascade reserve, will not be without value. In general, the progress of sheep grazing in the Cascades has been from the north toward the so.th and from the eastern toward the western slope. The areas over which grazing is likely to extend in the immediate future are westward and southward from the Three Sisters on the west slope and southward to some extent from the Diamond Lake area on the eastern slope. This extension will not be rapid, provided the number of sheep to be pastured in the Cascades does not continue to increase. If the number does increase and all the present available areas become overgrazed, fires are almost sure to occur in areas now well timbered—fires which are not countenanced by the best element of stockmen, but which will be caused by irresponsible packers and herders.

A general belief prevails that the increasing value of wool and mutton will cause an important and conspicuous increase in the number of sheep and that the summer grazing land will in a few years become overgrazed. This conclusion at first sight appears plausible, but it must be remembered that Oregon is a country on which other parts of the United States draw very largely for their lambs, and as the demand for stock sheep is on the increase and will probably continue to increase for some years, it is unquestionable that a large part of the expected increase in eastern Oregon will quickly leave the State. So fully and reasonably were the probable results of these fluctuations of the market and their effect upon stock sheep explained to me by a prominent owner in eastern Oregon, Mr. J. N. Williamson, of Prineville. that I am disposed to accept his judgment that within the next few years the number of sheep in eastern Oregon will not materially increase, but that, succeeding this period of a large outside demand for stock sheep, an overproduction in Oregon will take place, so that at the end of, say, four or five years a marked increase will probably have shown itself.

In this connection it may be said that an increase of the available range, should the demand for range increase, seems not impracticable. Under the peculiar conditions that exist in the lodgepole pine forests on the pumice soils of the southern portion of the sheep range (described on page 39), there seems to be no reason why, under a system of intelligent and skilled forest management, experiments can not be made. It seems probable that the forage output of Crane Prairie, for example, might be doubled; but the experiment must be conducted with great care and the effects carefully watched by measuring the run-off of the main fork of the Deschutes.

REMEDIAL MEASURES.

Two extreme remedies have been proposed for the present unstable and unsatisfactory system—namely, on the one side the total exclusion of sheep and on the other the abolition of the reserve.

EXCLUSION OF SHEEP FROM THE RESERVE.

Assuming that the Interior Department adopts and puts into execution the policy of exclusion, the evils incident to overgrazing would, of course, be prevented. But what would be the effect on the forest fires? Would they cease? If they would, and if exclusion were the only remedy that would bring this about, no question could fairly be raised against it. But from the facts that destructive fires occurred in the Cascades long before they were used as a sheep range, that destructive fires have occurred in parts of the reserve in which sheep have never grazed, and that destructive fires are to-day occurring from a variety of causes that have no connection with sheep grazing, it can not be maintained that exclusion of sheep would wholly stop the forest fires.

DIFFICULTIES BETWEEN SHEEPMEN AND RANCHERS.

One common and persistent source of opposition to the grazing of sheep in the reserve is the ranchers who live along the routes over which the sheep customarily pass as they are driven to and from the mountains. These ranchers own plots, comparatively small in most cases, of fenced arable land, taken up for the most part under the homestead act and commonly, therefore, containing 160 acres. The fenced area is not sufficiently large, in addition to the land under cultivation, to furnish pasturage for the few horses and cows required to work the ranch and supply milk and butter. Their only pasturage resource, therefore—for under the existing land laws they can neither buy nor lease any more land from the Government—is to run their stock upon the outside range. Between one rancher and another the customary range of his neighbor, though he has no title to it, is respected. But many of the sheep herders, not all, in driving their bands toward the mountains in spring, when the new grass is in excellent condition, without the slightest consideration for the rancher, and often, doubtless, to pay back a score of an earlier year's quarrel, will drive their sheep up to the very fences, and the grass may be eaten off so close that for the remainder of the season a cow can not get a nibble. There is no law, except the questionable law of the Winchester, by which the rancher can defend his home, and he earnestly supports the demand for exclusion, believing that if the sheep are kept out of the mountains the industry would be ruined and his own little range left free. The writer is confident, however, that this expected result would not be effected by exclusion, but that the sheep would be crowded into the lower range and the difficulty, except in a few favorably situated places, would be increased.

A remedy, and perhaps the most easily available one, has been suggested in the form of local legislation, prescribing limits (say a distance of half a mile) within which a band of sheep shall not be driven toward a ranch.

DIFFICULTIES BETWEEN SHEEPMEN AND CATTLEMEN.

Under the present land laws any man has a right to graze any amount of any kind of stock on any portion of the public lands (forest, Indian, and military reserves and national parks excepted) at any time. Naturally, sheep are very close grazers, and an area on which they are pastured can not be used for either cattle or horses. "They won't work together." Furthermore, sheep are herded stock, while cattle and horses are never herded. As a result, a sheep owner can drive his sheep to any portion of the public range he may select, and can therefore exercise essentially a prior right to any choice piece of grazing land and exclude all other stockmen from it. The only limit to a sheep owner's progress over the public range is, first, mutual consent between himself and his stock-grazing neighbors as to limits; second, the use of physical force. Between reasonable men mutual consent is usually effective. Between men who can not come to an agreement various discouragements are adopted, such as poisoning sheep by scattering on the ground castor-oil beans, or saltpeter mixed with salt, burning up the sheep-herder's camp when he is away herding his sheep, or opening fire on a band with buckshot or bullets. Occasionally these amenities end in the death of one or more men by shooting. Details of such cases need not be given here.

It is an interesting and important fact, however, that, whatever the difficulties between cattlemen and sheepmen regarding winter ranges in the plains, they are agreed in desiring the summer-range privilege for sheep in the mountains, the sheepmen, of course, from its distinct addition to their grazing opportunities, the cattlemen because the temporary removal of sheep from the plains leaves a larger amount of summer forage there for their own stock, particularly in the canyons and moist bottom lands.

OTHER DIFFICULTIES.

According to the statistics given earlier in the report. 101,960 sheep were grazed last year in the Three Sisters and the Upper Deschutes range districts. It appears from examination of the original data that of these sheep only 8,660 were owned in Crook County, all the others being owned in the counties of Wasco and Sherman. Now as the only routes to the Three Sisters and the Upper Deschutes districts are through Crook County, it follows that 93,300 sheep not owned in Crook County, and paying no taxes there, were driven across that county, eating up a large amount of forage that otherwise would have been available for the stock raisers of the county and causing damage to the roads, which must be repaired at the expense of the taxpayers of the county. The most practicable and direct remedy for this appears to lie not in excluding sheep from the reserve, but in levying on the transient sheep owners a county toll tax offsetting the amount of damage sustained by the county. This has been done in Inyo County, Cal., and doubtless elsewhere. The legislative functions of the counties of Oregon are extremely limited constitutionally, but the State could undoubtedly make the necessary enactment to remedy both this and the preceding difficulties.

Reference has already been made to a general opposition to sheep grazing in the reserve on the part of those who look upon the reserve as a park, to be withheld from the general use of the public, instead of a reservation of natural resources to be maintained in a state of the highest continued production. Congress by its legislation has repudiated this park idea of the forest reserves as a whole, but has made it possible to provide for the maintenance as parks of such portions as are admittedly suitable for this purpose and are demanded as such by the local or general public.

It is important to consider what would be the effect of exclusion on the trade relations and commercial welfare of the State of Oregon. Of the wool clip (that is, the wool product) of 1897 there had been sold up to September 1 at The Dalles alone, the principal shipping point for eastern Oregon, about 8,000,000 pounds at an average of 11 cents per pound, amounting to $880,000. To this must be added the sale of mutton and stock sheep, the statistics of which are not available. Of the three principal products of eastern Oregon, wool, beef, and wheat, it is a matter of common belief, frequently expressed, that the money that comes into the hands of woolgrowers is the most important as ready cash in the community; that the nature of the business is such as to make it a quick distributor of money and to add in a very material way to the general prosperity. According to the State census of Oregon for 1895 the wool clip of Crook County, for example, in that year was 1,983,325 pounds. Taking 15 cents as an average price, this amounts to $297,498.75. When it is considered that the population of Crook County, according to the census of 1895, was only 3,212, and that therefore the wool clip alone brings into the county an average of about $92.62 per capita each year, the importance of the wool-growing business as a supporter of local prosperity is at once evident. As a specific illustration of the significance of these figures, the following citations are presented from the Massachusetts State census and statistics of manufactures for 1895: population of Massachusetts, 2,500,183; manufactures of cotton goods, $86,689,082; of boots and shoes, $76,882,713; food preparations, $43,984,375; machines and machinery, $23,785,409. The total product of these manufacturing industries, the largest in the State of Massachusetts, is $231,341,579, an average of $92.53 per capita. In brief, the wool clip alone in Crook County is of as much commercial importance to its people as the five largest manufacturing industries of Massachusetts combined are to the people of that State. Crook County is for its population a large purchaser of general merchandise, most of which is either produced in the Willamette Valley or is shipped from outside the State through Portland. The prosperity of Crook County, therefore, is of importance to the prosperity of the whole State. Similar trade relations, varying in each case, exist in most of the thirteen other counties of eastern Oregon. Both the men who make laws and the men who administer them must weigh carefully the effect of their action before striking a blow at one of the leading industries of a region, such as would be struck in the present case by excluding sheep from the reserve. Many ranchers and other men who have a dislike of sheep, of the methods of some sheep owners, and of the devastating effect of overgrazing, nevertheless stated that in their opinion the exclusion of sheep from the reserve was against the best commercial interests of their communities.

ABOLITION OF THE RESERVE.

The proposition, on the other extreme, to abolish the Cascade Reserve originated with the sheep owners and doubtless did a great deal to foster the general public opinion that the sheep owners were carrying on an industry opposed to the best interests of the State. It has always been a matter of surprise to me that the sheep owners, instead of taking the almost inevitably untenable stand that the reserve be not established, did not, rather, favor the reserve, but demand that the right to graze be conceded to them. This is now explained. I was reliably informed by leading sheep owners that they were misled by a prominent official who supposed, and accordingly so told them, that if the reserve was created sheep would undoubtedly be excluded. Under these circumstances they took the only course open to them, namely, to advocate the maintenance of the then existing conditions by opposing the creation of the reserve. From conversations with representative sheep owners the writer is convinced that a large majority of them, if they are given the grazing privilege on equitable terms, will cordially accept the reserve as a public benefit.

A NEW SYSTEM OF REGULATIONS.

After a thorough examination of the whole subject of sheep grazing in the Cascade reserve the writer's conclusions are that the evils of the present system can be corrected neither on the one side by abolishing the reserve nor on the other side by the exclusion of sheep, without inflicting much more serious evils upon the welfare of the State. But a system can be adopted which, honestly and intelligently carried out, will stop the real evils of the present system and at the same time maintain the interests of all the communities concerned.

The first step toward a satisfactory system of sheep-grazing regulations in the Cascade reserve is to provide absolute protection for those places which the people of the State require as public resorts or for reservoir purposes. The grandeur of the natural scenery of the Cascades is coming to be better known. Even before the forest reserve was created a movement was on foot to have the Mount Hood region and the Crater Lake region set aside as national parks, and since the reserve was created the eminent desirability and propriety of the earlier movement has been clearly recognized, both in the continued efforts of the people to keep sheep from grazing in these regions and in the concession in the petition of the sheep owners that if the Cascade reserve as a whole be abolished the Crater Lake and Mount Hood regions should be maintained as smaller and separate reserves on which sheep be not allowed to graze. In the tentative regulations of the General Land Office, dated June 30, 1897, the justice of these representations was officially recognized by a rule excluding sheep from grazing "upon or in the vicinity of the Bull Run Reserve [a small reservoir reserve contiguous to the Cascade reserve at its northwestern extremity], Crater Lake, Mount Hood, Mount Rainier [in another reserve in the State of Washington], or other well known places of public resort or reservoir supply." Before this exclusion can be made effective the exact limits of the areas specified must be described by metes and bounds and the boundaries marked.

Crater Lake.—How much should be included in the closed areas at Mount Hood and Crater Lake is a question to which considerable attention was paid in the field. After going twice carefully over the ground at Crater Lake and consulting with various men well informed on the subject, especially Capt. O. C. Applegate. of Klamath Falls, the writer questions whether a better area can be adopted than that covered by the special Crater Lake contour map, published by the United States Geological Survey. which extends from longitude 122° to 122° 15', and from latitude 42° 50' to 43° 4'. At present no sheep are grazed in the vicinity of Crater Lake, but for a few years. up to and including 1896, a small amount of summer grazing was carried on in the watershed of Anna Creek and that of the upper Rogue River.

Mount Hood.—It was our intention to submit a report on suitable boundaries for the closed area about Mount Hood, but as various petitions and memorials on the subject have been presented directly to the Secretary of the Interior and are under consideration, no recommendations are here submitted. It may be well to state, however, that three principal propositions have been made as to the boundaries of the proposed closure. In the order of their size, beginning with the smallest, they are as follows: (1) two roughly triangular blocks. one extending from the summit of Mount Hood north to the edge of the reserve. bounded on the east by the East Fork of Hood River and on the west by the Bull Run reserve, the other extending from the summit of Mount Hood southward to the boundary between townships 3 and 4 south, bounded on the east by White River and on the west by Zigzag Creek and the line between ranges 7 and 8 east; (2) all that portion of the reserve north of the Barlow road and west of the summit of the divide east of the East Fork of Hood River; (3) all that portion of the reserve north of an east-and-west line drawn through the northern boundary of the Warm Springs Indian Reservation.

Huckleberry patches.—In this connection one of Oregon's peculiar institutions should not be lost sight of. This is the practice common to the ranchers and townspeople who live near the Cascade Range of resorting to the mountains in summer to pick huckleberries. There are areas in the mountains which from late August to October produce annually an enormous amount of wild huckleberries (chiefly the kind known to botanists as *Vaccinium membranaceum*), and the present inhabitants, following an aboriginal custom of the Indians, go into the mountains, usually a whole family together, often driving 100 miles, and camp out for a few weeks, hunting, fishing, and picking huckleberries. One such area, known as Huckleberry Mountain, lies about 12 miles southwest of Crater Lake, immediately south of Union Creek, an affluent of Rogue River. It is not included within the boundaries of the proposed closed area at Crater Lake, described above, and should ultimately be made a closed area. Immense huckleberry patches are situated on and immediately south of Mount Hood, and should be taken into consideration in defining the closed area of that vicinity. Another favorite huckleberry patch lies on the west slope of the Cascades south of the Santiam-Prineville road, but it was not visited by the party, nor was its exact location ascertained.

Finally, with reference to closed areas, as the population of Oregon increases the recreation of the people will require the setting aside of additional areas of resort from which sheep must be excluded. No place will be attractive as a public resort if the vegetation is eaten off every year by sheep, nor can camping parties, under such circumstances, find suitable pasturage for their horses.

GRAZING PERMITS.

The system of regulations here proposed, which may be called the "special-tract permit system," is, in brief, the granting of the grazing privilege to sheep owners in return for the protection of the reserve from forest fires and overgrazing. It is proposed to grant to each owner a permit to graze on a specified territory a certain number of sheep, such as that area can support without detriment; to give him the exclusive right to graze on that area; and to protect him in that right; at the same time requiring on his part that he confine himself to that area; fulfill all the terms of his agreement with the Government;

and especially that he keep the area free, so far as lies within his power, from forest fires.

As an illustration I may cite the Fish Lake range in the Three Sisters range district. This range is divided into five smaller ranges, known as The Parks, Bald Mountain, Iron Mountain, Browder Ridge, and the Blue River range. These altogether will support, without overgrazing, six bands averaging 2,000 each, one band upon each of the first four, two bands upon the last. In 1896 there were eight bands on the Fish Lake range, two of them on The Parks, one on Bald Mountain, one on Iron Mountain, the other four on Browder Ridge and the Blue River range, alternating one or two on the former and three or two on the latter. This was a larger number of sheep than the Fish Lake range could support properly, and as a result the sheep did not all come out in good condition and there was general dissatisfaction among the owners. By the adoption of the system here proposed, the number of sheep allowed on the Fish Lake range would be limited to 12,000. No other sheep would be permitted to go into the Fish Lake range. Each owner would be assigned that subdivision of the range on which he had been accustomed to run his sheep, and would be supported and defended in his exclusive right to graze there. In return, it would be the duty of the owner occupying Browder Ridge to see that no forest fires be allowed to occur on that area, either those set carelessly and intentionally by his own herder or packer, or those set by any hunter, camper, or other person who might be on that territory. If forest fires did occur on Browder Ridge and the Interior Department was satisfied that the owner or his employees had not made every reasonable effort to prevent them or, when once started, to extinguish them, his permit would be terminated forthwith, and if evidence of collusion in setting the fires were shown, one or all of the persons concerned would still be liable to prosecution under the forest-fire laws.

ADVANTAGES TO THE GOVERNMENT AND THE SHEEP OWNER.

To the Government the chief advantage of such a system would be to prevent a very large proportion of the fires that occur in the sheep-grazing area. The enormous annual loss in burned timber would at once be checked. By the granting of a permit for a particular area, the responsibility of the owner is direct and his sense of that responsibility is keen. Under the old system an owner may range anywhere, with any number of sheep, and the Government knows neither where he is nor what he is doing.

The advantages to the sheep owner are several and important. The adage, "Every man for himself and the devil take the hindermost," was never more justly applicable to any business than to this one of grazing sheep on the public lands. It is to the interest of each owner to get his sheep sheared as early in the season as possible, even before the cold weather is gone. in order to get them off to the mountains before his neighbor. Then he must make long drives so as to keep ahead. and if his range lies on the west slope of the Cascades he will drive across the summit while it is yet covered with snow, the sheep passing sometimes two and even three days on the snow drifts without a nibble of grass. Then he has reached his range first, and is reasonably secure for the season. But the ground is still soft. the spring rains may still be falling. and the sprouting grass has not yet reached the development necessary to make good feed. He may be crowded off during the summer. though usually it does not pay a later arrival to push in on a range already occupied. Whatever happens. it is usually to the owner's interest to get all the grass possible without reference to the next year's crop. for he is never certain that he will be able to occupy the same range again. Where the competition is close the difficulty of insufficient forage is increased by the haste of a herder in forcing his sheep too rapidly over a grazing plot, the result being that they trample more feed than they eat. So year after year each band skins the range.

Under the proposed permit system, however, the owner, knowing that his range is assured, will shear his sheep at the time best suited by the local climatic conditions for that purpose, and will start for the mountains at a reasonable time. This is a matter of especial importance to those owners who live on the higher elevations of the plain, 3,000 feet or more above the sea, and who, in order to be in the race with those living at an elevation of 1,000 feet or less, must ordinarily under existing conditions leave their home range two weeks too early, at a time when it still bears a profusion of fresh, nutritious grass. Reaching the grazing areas in the mountains when the grass has grown to a fair degree of maturity a larger amount of better forage awaits the packer, and with a definite knowledge that he will use the same area in the following year, he so handles his sheep as not to permanently injure the grass. Indeed, he may find it profitable to improve it by seeding with good varieties of clover and grass. One owner stated that several years ago he had sowed one summer $20 worth of clover and grass seed, but that never having been able to secure the same range again he got no benefit from his expenditure and had discontinued all efforts in that direction. With an assured title for a period of years an owner can also put up substantial shelters for his men and their provisions. A further advantage of great importance to sheep owners is the circumstance that, lying within a forest reserve, the grazing lands are not subject to homestead entry, and no one, therefore, by securing a title to the land, can prevent its use as a sheep range. By a judicious use of the privilege granted under the proposed system the grazing lands of the reserve become a perpetual sheep range. To both the State itself and to the general body of sheep owners the proposed system is an advantage, from the evident fact that if the forest grazing privilege is valuable at all. it is most valuable when the amount of forage it furnishes is maintained at its highest limit of continued production, as would be the case under the proposed system, instead of being maintained at its lowest limit of production, as would finally be the case under the present system.

There is a popular but erroneous idea that the responsibility for the present system of grazing in eastern Oregon rests with the sheep owners. It is found, however, on conversation with a large number of them that they are opposed to the present method, and would welcome a change in government policy which would give them a financial interest in the maintenance of good pasturage. If they could secure for a reasonable period of years a title to the grazing product they believe it would be one of the greatest benefits possible to the industry.

OBJECTIONS TO THE PROPOSED SYSTEM.

In discussing the proposed plan with stockmen it was found, somewhat unexpectedly, that all those to whom there was opportunity of explaining it fully, without exception approved it, but often with the proviso, "if it could be carried out." Their primary doubt was that though a majority of the owners would gladly adopt the system, there would always be a few who would refuse to agree to any regulations or would be unscrupulous enough to trangress them when they found it to their own interest to do so. It appears that the eminent desirability of adopting some scheme of parceling out the range had long been recognized and in an informal way had been attempted in various localities, but that invariably some unscrupulous owner, by crowding in upon another's range, had broken up the system.

Upon being reminded that a new set of laws had been enacted, under which the Interior Department had full authority to make regulations covering the land within the forest reserves and full power to enforce them, and that while the Government undoubtedly wished to handle the subject with the velvet hand of equity there lay beneath it the iron claw of stern authority, they readily appreciated that recalcitrant owners would not be so serious an obstacle to the Interior Department as they had been to their own unauthorized system.

A second objection, and one at first difficult to meet, was that the Interior Department would be unable to divide the range equitably; that certain owners, particularly large owners, would secure the best ranges, and that continued dissatisfaction would result. The objection clearly was well made. The writer had been keeping a list of all the ranges, with the number of sheep each would support, and knew how extremely difficult it would be for any one man to do full justice to each individual owner, especially in the face of the conflicting representations with which he would be met. The Northern Pacific Railroad and other corporations having grazing privileges to dispose of can, and do, deal directly with individual applicants without necessarily consulting others, but this method is not open to the Government. The most natural way to decide between two or more persons competing for the same right is to grant it to the highest bidder. Doubts of the suitability of this method were confirmed by conversations with various people. The unanimous verdict was that such a proceeding would tend to put the grazing lands in the hands of a small number of large owners who could afford to pay a higher price than owners of single bands.

As a result of careful consideration the plan of permitting the sheep owners themselves to parcel out the range suggested itself. It was found that in each of the three counties concerned—Crook, Wasco, and Sherman—there exists a woolgrowers' or stockmen's association, the original object of which, it appeared, was chiefly mutual protection of their sheep against coyotes and other wild animals through the payment of bounties raised by subscription or tax among the members of the association. A committee or commission of three, each representing one of these county associations, would be thoroughly competent to divide the range, and could do it both more equitably and with less objection from dissatisfied owners than could any officer or officers of the Government. This commission could meet at a time and place duly advertised, receive the written applications for range, adjudicate conflicting applications, and make recommendations accordingly to the Interior Department. This plan answered the last objection brought forward against the system.

ADDITIONAL DETAILS.

Other details of the system may be briefly mentioned. The permit should be for a definite number of years, sufficient to give the permittee an interest in maintaining the range in good productive condition from year to year, and on the other hand it should not be for so long a period as to prevent new men from coming into the business. A permit period of five years with a provision for renewal appears to be the most satisfactory.

Failure on the part of a permittee to occupy a range before the expiration of a reasonable period, say by the 1st of August in any year, without due explanation, would cause the permit to lapse and the range to be again open to application and the granting of a new permit for the rest of the season and the remaining portion of the original term. This would prevent any owner from wasting the resources to which he might have an exclusive right.

The suggestion has been made by a citizen of Oregon that a sheep owner, as one of the requisites for obtaining a permit, should give a bond securing the Government against destruction of the timber by fire. This provision, however, would be a hardship in many cases and should be adopted only as a last resort. Another provision, the adoption of which is worth considering, is the exclusion of sheep for a period of several years, or until the seedlings are too high to be trampled, from any piece of forest land hereafter burned. The object of this would be: first, to allow the seedlings to get a good start; secondly, to remove the temptation to set a forest fire for the purpose of creating new range.

It is essential that provision should be made for those cases in which an owner, in order to reach the tract allotted to him, must cross a tract allotted to another owner. After careful consideration, the simplest and most effective means of control appears to be to provide for a right of transit with a minimum rate of travel per day. This rate should be between 7 and 10 miles, perhaps the most suitable rate, all things considered, being 8 miles. At the same time, the owner whose tract is crossed should have received an original allotment sufficiently large to compensate him for the amount of feed that would be used by the one or more bands that have the right of transit.

If provision is made by Congress for a forest reserve service and an adequate system of administration, an adjustment of the officers can easily be made by which the proper carrying out of the proposed permit system may be assured, but it may not be amiss to point out that upon the integrity and ability of these officers rests in large measure the success of the system.

FEES AND COST OF ADMINISTRATION.

The Government will be subjected to some expense in the administration of the permit plan, and the cost of this administration should be borne by the sheep owners, to be paid in the form of a fee for the permit.

ABSTRACT OF PROPOSED REGULATIONS.

In order to sum up the conclusions of this investigation in a form showing concisely what action should be taken by the Interior Department to inaugurate a satisfactory system for the regulation of sheep grazing in the Cascade reserve, an abstract of the proposed plan is given below. It must not be forgotten that this report, both in the matter of the extent of damage done to the forests by sheep and in the system proposed for its regulation, applies only to sheep grazing in the Cascade Range Forest Reserve, and that very different findings of fact and propositions for regulation might have been submitted had the area in question been situated under different climatic conditions, or had it contained other types of soil or other kinds of forests, or had been subject to sheep grazing for a longer period, or had other equally important conditions affected the problem.

The steps necessary to a solution of present difficulties by the Interior Department are as follows, and these steps, in order to save and perpetuate the timber supply and the water supply of middle Oregon, should be taken at once:

1. Exclude sheep from specified areas about Mount Hood and Crater Lake.

2. Limit the sheep to be grazed in the reserve to a specified number based on the number customarily grazing there.

3. Issue five-year permits allowing an owner to graze sheep on a specified tract. limiting the number of sheep to be grazed on that tract, and giving the owner the exclusive grazing right.

4. Require as a condition of each permit that the owner use every effort to prevent and to extinguish fires on his tract, and report in full the cause. extent, and other circumstances connected with each fire.

5. Reserve the right to terminate a permit immediately if convinced that an owner is not showing good faith in the protection of the forests.

6. In the allotment of tracts secure the cooperation of the wool growers' associations of Crook, Sherman. and Wasco counties through a commission of three stockmen. who shall receive written applications for range. adjudicate them, and make recommendations, these recommendations to be reviewed by the forest officer and finally passed upon by the Secretary of the Interior.

7. Ask the county associations to bear the expenses of the commission.

8. Charge the cost of administration of the system to the owners in the form of fees for the permits.

9. If the wool growers decline to accept and to cooperate in the proposed system, exclude sheep absolutely from the reserve.

10. If. after five years' trial of the system. forest fires continue unchecked, exclude sheep thereafter from the reserve.

○

www.ingramcontent.com/pod-product-compliance
Lightning Source LLC
Chambersburg PA
CBHW021639270326
41931CB00008B/1080